FROM ZERO
TO
THE ABSOLUTE

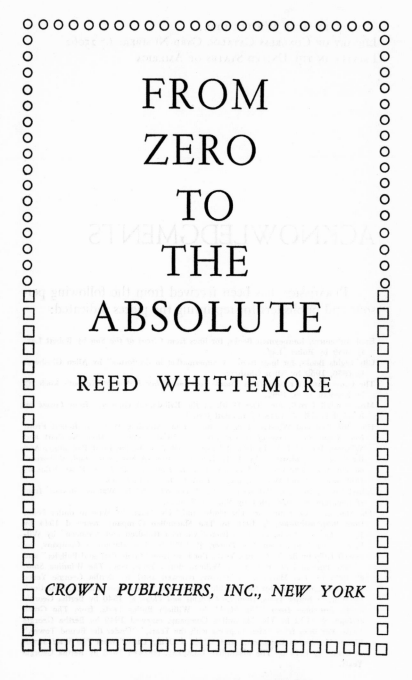

FROM
ZERO
TO
THE
ABSOLUTE

REED WHITTEMORE

CROWN PUBLISHERS, INC., NEW YORK

ACKNOWLEDGMENTS

Permission has been received from the following persons and publishers for reprinting the pieces indicated:

Emil Antonucci, Journeyman Books, for lines from *Circus of the Sun* by Robert Lax. © 1959 by Robert Lax.

City Lights Books, for lines from "A Supermarket in California" by Allen Ginsberg. © 1956, 1959 by Allen Ginsberg.

The Grove Press for lines from *Thank You and Other Poems* by Kenneth Koch. © by Kenneth Koch, 1962.

Mrs. Randall Jarrell, for "The Death of the Ball-Turret Gunner," from *Losses* by Randall Jarrell. © 1948 by Randall Jarrell.

Holt, Rinehart and Winston, Inc., for lines from "Mending Wall" by Robert Frost, from *Complete Poems of Robert Frost*, © 1930, 1939, by Holt, Rinehart and Winston, Inc. © 1958 by Robert Frost. © 1967 by Lesley Frost Ballantine. And for "The New Mistress" by A. E. Housman, from *A Shropshire Lad*, authorized edition, from *The Collected Poems of A. E. Housman*. © 1939, 1940, 1959 by Holt, Rinehart and Winston, Inc. © 1967 by Robert E. Symons.

Alfred Knopf, Inc., for "Disillusionment of Ten o'Clock" by Wallace Stevens, from *Harmonium*, © 1923 1931 by Wallace Stevens.

The Macmillan Company for "The Dolls" and "The Magi" by William Butler Yeats, from *Responsibilities*, © 1916 by The Macmillan Company, renewed 1944 by Bertha Georgie Yeats. For lines from "Nineteen Hundred and Nineteen" by William Butler Yeats, from *The Tower*, © 1928 by The Macmillan Company, renewed 1956 by Bertha Georgie Yeats. For lines from "Coole Park and Ballylee" and "Crazy Jane and the Bishop" by William Butler Yeats, from *The Winding Stair*, © 1933 by The Macmillan Company, renewed 1961 by Bertha Georgie Yeats. For lines from "News for the Delphic Oracle" and "The Circus Animals' Desertion" by William Butler Yeats, from *Last Poems and Plays*, © 1940 by Bertha Georgie Yeats. For lines from "The Mask" by William Butler Yeats, from *The Green Helmet*, © 1912 by The Macmillan Company, renewed 1940 by Bertha Georgie Yeats. For lines from "Men Improve with the Years," "Under the Round Tower," "Lines Written in Dejection," and "Upon a Dying Lady," from *The Wild Swans at Coole*, © 1919 by The Macmillan Company, renewed 1946 by Bertha Georgie Yeats.

Mrs. Edgar Lee Masters, for lines from "Petit the Poet" by Edgar Lee Masters, from *Spoon River Anthology*, © 1914, 1915, 1916 by Edgar Lee Masters.

Howard Nemerov for "A Spell Before Winter," by Howard Nemerov, from *The Next Room of the Dream*, © 1962 by Howard Nemerov. And for excerpts from *Journal of the Fictive Life*, by Howard Nemerov, © 1965 by Howard Nemerov.

New Directions Publishing Corporation, for lines from "Dulce et Docorum Est" by Wilfred Owen, from *The Collected Poems of Wilfred Owen*, © by Chatto & Windus, Ltd., 1963. And for lines from "Homage to Sextus Propertius" by Ezra Pound, from *Personae*, © 1926 by Ezra Pound. And for lines from "The Third Dimension" by Denise Levertov, from *With Eyes at the Back of Our Heads*, © 1958 by Denise Levertov Goodman. And for lines from "In a Surrealist Year" by Lawrence Ferlinghetti, from *A Coney Island of the Mind*, © 1958 by Lawrence Ferlinghetti. And for lines from *The Very Thing That Happens* by Russell Edson, © 1963 by Russell Edson. And for "The Red Wheelbarrow" by William Carlos Williams, from *The Collected Earlier Poems* of William Carlos Williams, © 1938, 1951 by William Carlos Williams.

Oxford University Press for a passage from *The Partial Critics* by Lee Lemon, © 1965 by Lee Lemon.

Random House, Inc., for lines from "Elegy for a Dead Soldier" by Karl Shapiro, .from *V-Letter and Other Poems*, © 1944 by Karl Jay Shapiro. And for "Lower the Standards" by Karl Shapiro, from *The Bourgeois Poet*, © 1962, 1963 by Karl Shapiro. And for lines from "In Memory of W. B. Yeats" by W. H. Auden, from *The Collected Poetry of W. H. Auden*, © 1945 by W. H. Auden.

The Viking Press, for "To Be Superior" by D. H. Lawrence, from *The Complete Poems of D. H. Lawrence*, edited by Vivian de Sola Pinto and F. Warren Roberts, © 1929 by Frieda Lawrence Ravagli.

Wesleyan University Press for "Lying in a Hammock at William Duffy's Farm in Pine Island, Minnesota" by James Wright, from *The Branch Will Not Break*, © 1961 by James Wright.

Yale University Press, for "Orpheus in Greenwich Village" by Jack Gilbert, from *Views of Jeopardy*, © 1962 by Yale University.

*   *   *

Acknowledgment is also made to *The Carleton Miscellany*, in which the essay "Poetry and Bureaucracy" first appeared.

"Wordsworth and Woman," "Today," "Dear God," "Aladdin's Genie" and "Lines Composed Upon Reading an Announcement by Civil Defense Authorities Recommending That I Build a Bombshelter in My Backyard" by Reed Whittemore appear in *Poems New & Selected*, University of Minnesota Press, © 1967 by Reed Whittemore. "White Cross," "Black Cross" and "God's Acres" by Reed Whittemore appear in *An American Takes a Walk*, University of Minnesota Press, © 1956 by Reed Whittemore.

88521

To Helen

To Helen

CONTENTS

CONTENTS

INTRODUCTION

FOR THE ECCENTRIC organizing principle behind the Beloit College lectures, which make up the first part of this volume, I'm indebted to Karl Shapiro. In 1963 Shapiro inaugurated the Ward Lucas lecture series at Carleton College by going alphabetically through the writers in his bookcase. I was impressed and became an immediate disciple—of the form.

But I decided that for my whirl with the form I'd go through the alphabet backward. I have. And rather than cataloguing writers as Shapiro did, I have dealt with concepts or places or things that somehow impinge upon modern poetry. Hence, under "Z," as you will see, I discuss Zero; under "A," later, the Absolute.

You may ask what virtue other than surprise attaches to the form. It is a random form, hence modern and fashionable. But it is also an undemanding form, easy to live with. I chose it not because it was fashionable but because it seemed livable. I felt that my subject was too big to be well methodized—the subject was given me: modern poetry—and that I had best acknowledge disunity at the start. Oddly, as I got further in, I began to think I was finding unity after all, maybe even monotony.

The lectures are not intended as a short course in modern poetry. I have taught modern poetry too long. My intention here was to get down a few things, partly for my own benefit, that haven't crept into the courses.

I want to thank my hosts at Beloit College, faculty, administration, and students, first for stirring me to compose the lectures, and second for being a most responsive audience for them. The occasion was a rare and exciting one for me.

The other lectures, appearing in Part II of this book, also have sponsors to whom I am most grateful. Lawrence University invited me to deliver "The Limitations of Reason" for Honors Day in 1964. The Library of Congress gave me a stage for "Ways of Misunderstanding Poetry," also in 1964. And Carleton College, San Francisco State College, Southwestern Louisiana University, and Emory and Henry College bent their ears to "Poetry and Bureaucracy" in 1965 and 1966. Then a kindly committee of the Modern Language Association permitted me to berate a roomful of English teachers at the annual MLA meeting in 1965, with "On Graduate Training in English, Yet." Finally, the lecture entitled "Poetry and the Skinner Box" was delivered as the first Bain-Swiggett lecture at Princeton in the spring of 1967; it is really a supplement to the four Beloit Lectures.

PART I

From Zero to the Absolute

1

FROM ZERO TO WAR

Z

zero

EVERY POEM, T. S. Eliot said, is a new start with shabby
equipment constantly deteriorating. Eliot was getting on
when he wrote those words, so his emphasis was on the deteriorating equipment. For youth, however, the stress is apt
to be on newness. And for the whole age of what we call
"modern poetry," the stress has been on newness. Each
poem is a new start. The poet sits at his desk without a
thought in his head, thinking he has thoughts in his head.
He writes. And if what he writes turns out to be as old as
the Rocky Mountains, still there was the moment before
writing when poetry, or the act of poetry, was newness,
strangeness, wonder, a venture into the unknown, a raid, as
Eliot put it, on the inarticulate.

Our culture continues to entertain high hopes for
poetry as an art, and it does so even though it is constantly
being submerged by dreadful poems. It does so on faith. It
keeps thinking that poetry can and will produce the newness and wonder it *ought* to produce. Take away the
"ought"; remove the conviction that a lonely man can sit at
a lonely desk with an empty head and conjure up a brave
new world, and suddenly the catalogue of man's hopes looks
depressingly slimmer.

Last year I saw an art exhibit in Washington called
"Zero." In it the artists to a man were reaching out for

3

newness and wonder by trying to start from scratch in their
art, by canceling out their artistic heritage, by putting themselves in the position of God in the Book of Genesis. It will
be one of my themes here—and a very simpleminded theme
it is—that no artist can start from scratch in his art, that
zero-hunting is a fallacy. But I don't propose to ignore it
because it's a fallacy. It's much too widespread a fallacy to
ignore. It's a whole cultural phenomenon. Call it "primitivism." Or call it "instant anthropology." In another age
it was Rousseauism. It seems to be produced by a reaction
against certain "givens" in an art and the art's society,
givens ranging from the forms, genres or conventions of the
art itself to the mountain of givens of the culture surround-
ing the art. How deep and far-reaching the reaction from
the givens has been among our modern poets is subject for
dispute, but certainly we are dealing with a phenomenon
far from trivial. Karl Shapiro, during lectures given at
Carleton College two years ago, said, "Almost to a man
American artists and writers are in full-fledged opposition
to the American Way of Life—that is, life according to
Business, Politics, Journalism, Advertising, Religion, Patriotism and Morality." That statement is what Shapiro
now calls a Shapiroism—not a half-truth but a one-and-a-
half truth—but even if we take it at a very substantial dis-
count, I think we can see the prime motive for modern
zero-hunting in our arts.

When the dissident artist, the artist in reaction, sets
out to make his raid on the inarticulate, he thinks he must
first dispose of what has already been articulated. He must
get rid of the false accretions of his society and culture
before he can make a start, an honest start, in his own work.
Creativity is only possible, he decides, after the striptease.
Even Robert Frost's work contains this kind of thinking—
see "Directive."

The other way of art, the nondissident way, the classical way, is to *add* to what has already been articulated. No

artist now under thirty seems to want to do that, and many over thirty don't want to either. One of the over-thirty dissidents, Charles Olson, sets the anticlassical tone well, and lucidly articulates a "zero" theory for poetry, in a popular recent anthology, *The New American Poetry, 1945–1960.* Olson is selling something that he calls "projective verse," and to get us to understand what projective verse is, he immediately takes us to the roots of things by complaining about traditional verse. Traditional verse is closed verse; it is governed or fenced in by all sorts of inherited systems or forms or coherences. What Olson proposes instead is open verse, what he calls "composition by field." He says that any poet who "departs from the closed form" is confronted by "a whole series of new recognitions. From the moment he ventures in FIELD COMPOSITION—puts himself in the open—he can go by no track other than the one the poem under hand declares, for itself."

There's the fallacy in the raw. No poem declares long for itself. The measure of freedom its author may achieve is relatively slight, and remains slight no matter how desirable the freedom may be. Yet this fallacy, first popularized, perhaps inadvertently, by Ezra Pound, and since then constantly repeated, has itself emerged as a cultural imperative, especially in our country. W. H. Auden once observed, while flying over Wyoming, that our country looks from the air like an open field literally—at least to an Englishman. He added that American poetry looks like Wyoming.

He should have gone back a bit further and said that American poetry looks like Walden Pond. American poets, even some very sophisticated poets like Pound and Cummings and now Shapiro, have believed with Thoreau that their connections with society are slight and ephemeral. They have felt a detachment from the culture, or at least a capacity for detachment, which is mostly not evident in their British counterparts. The freedom of American poetry is special; it is the freedom to think with other American poets that one is free. Christian Science.

Once born, we are not free to return to zero until we die. Zero-hunting not only goes against the old classical view of art; it goes against psychology and sociology and anthropology and all the "ologies," as well as against maturity and life itself. This does not mean, however, that zero-hunting is merely futile and ridiculous. If an artist keeps hard at his zero-hunting he will not get to zero, but he will at least arrive somewhere else than where the society is. He will get to a point quite removed from what I will call—to sound scientific—the "cultural median." That is, he will get way out in left field.

So much for "Z" and zero.

Y

yaddo and yale

"Y" stands for Yaddo and Yale. Yaddo is an artists' colony near Saratoga. I have never been there but have spent parts of two summers with Yaddo's rival, the MacDowell Colony in New Hampshire. At MacDowell one talks constantly of Yaddo: Yaddo is richer than MacDowell; Yaddo has a swimming pool; one dresses for dinner at Yaddo.

I have been to Yale. Yale is a critic's colony. Yale has at least three swimming pools: the proper modern ratio between criticism and art.

It's best for a professing poet like me to make small jokes about institutions. If he doesn't, someone will say he has sold out—and maybe they will anyway. Our Wyoming lore tells us the poet must be Daniel Boone in Paris, the critic, his roommate. Genius and good taste, says the lore, can't live with institutions. As Ezra Pound observed to the Alumni Secretary of the University of Pennsylvania in 1929, "All the U. of P. or your goddam college or any other goddam college does or will do for a man of letters is to ask him to go away without breaking the silence."

Both Yale and Yaddo reek a bit of money and decorum, but they will still do nicely to represent institutional benevolence toward dissident, separatist artists. At Yale poetry is studied and taught; at Yaddo it is writ. At both it is treated with reverence; both are congenial institutions at which to be outraged by institutions. There are many institutions like them, and they effectively refute the Wyoming argument that the poet is safe only outside them. At Yaddo the poet is left alone, stuck with himself, for just as long as he can stand it. At Yale or any other good university the poet or critic, be he teacher or student, is given a chance he will simply not find elsewhere, to immerse himself in literature to the ears. And though he may not find time at Yale during the school year to write his own world literature, he can drive off to Yaddo in the summer and write it. In an institutional age the artist's best bet would seem to be not to try to escape institutions but to ally himself with institutions that like him.

But there is a catch, and the catch is as much the fault of the artists as of the institutions. In a way the artists and the institutions are collaborating to do art in, not by institutionalizing it, as Pound and so many of his successors fear, but by positively encouraging its separatism, its zero-hunting propensities.

Let me explain by digressing slightly. I think it is the assumption of most poets that poetry at its best deals with the whole range of human thought and that poets at their best are well *ahead* of their culture's thinking. The assumption is pretentious, but it is with us. These recent words by Conrad Aiken display it well:

Poetry has always kept easily abreast with the utmost man can do in extending the horizon of his consciousness, whether outward or inward. It has always been the most flexible, the most comprehensive, the most farseeing, and hence the most successful of the modes by which he has accepted the new in experience, realized it, and adjusted himself to it.

I find that statement eloquent but wrong. Poetry has not kept abreast, though poets have seemed to want to. Poetry has not been flexible, comprehensive, and farseeing, though poets have wanted it to be. Mr. Aiken has expressed the ideal, not the fact of our art, and this is a distinction that poets and institutions have collaborated upon in our time to blur. Our benevolent institutions have created a refuge from comprehensiveness, farseeingness; and the artists have jumped at it. Only the rare poet nowadays thinks of his art as an adjunct to anything; it is the whole hog. And the institutions with which he allies himself either agree with him or are willing to go along with him by providing conditions under which he can think it is the whole hog. The critics, meanwhile, safely ensconced in their halls of graduate studies, strengthen the poet's notion of self-sufficiency by churning out grand new *doctrines* of artistic self-sufficiency (doctrines I'll go into later). On this over-whelmingly important point there seems to be no disagreement among poets, critics, and administrators. Yet this is exactly where disagreement needs to flourish. Even as broad-minded a critic as Lionel Trilling can be found asserting that "of course literature is independent." When he said this, the "of course" was fortunately ironic, meaning, "of course it is understood in the halls of the literary establishment that literature is independent"; but even so, that "of course" is a big one, and among the more determined advocates of an autotelic literature the "of courses" appear with no irony.

Especially when they are applied to poetry. Poetry has been the fall-guy art here. One recent critic, Lee Lemon, for example, in a book called *The Partial Critics*, has worked up a whole new book of literary theory, using only lyric poetry as a base, on the grounds that lyric poetry brings us hard up against problems of literary theory in their purity as no other kind of literature does. He says:

Lyric poetry seems a likely place to begin a theory of literature because the individual works are relatively manageable and because the lyric raises the basic questions of literary theory. What is the relationship between form and meaning? What kind of "truth," if any, does literature possess? What is the nature of aesthetic experience? What is the relationship between the author and his work? The lyric raises these and similar questions in comparative purity. That is, there are many valid and sufficient nonliterary defenses of, say, *Macbeth* or *Crime and Punishment*; it is much harder to invent nonliterary defenses of Keats' "Ode to Autumn."

I think Mr. Lemon is right, depressingly right; it *is* easier to construct literary theories around poetry than around novels and plays. It is also easier for the poet than for the playwright or the novelist to ply his trade in the isolation of Yale and Yaddo without ever thinking about anything except his art. Perhaps this very ease has been the chief cause of the present conspiracy between critics and poets, a conspiracy to kill poetry by making it free, free of the culture, the world.

One other word on the conspiracy. It is apt to thrive at the very best colleges or in the most respected writers' nooks, that is, at the institutions that take most pride in their standards. The easy way to be sure of having high standards is to eliminate, arbitrarily, the nasty problems of the validity of the standards, to take the logical positivist position that here, here, and here are the boundaries of our art, our department, our province, beyond which we will not go. Adopting such a position is a great convenience, as Mr. Lemon pointed out; and it is also a sound disciplinary procedure for the scholar or craftsman. As soon as an English Department starts to go interdisciplinary, there go the standards. As soon as a poet gets "engaged," there goes his integrity. And so on.

But as a small critical aside I must say that at Carleton College *for example* (I will not presume to speak of Beloit on such short acquaintance), the strengths of having high standards and preserving departmental integrity and curricular integrity, all that—the strengths keep looking more and more like weaknesses to me. The shiftiness of what we need to have standards *for* is what we neglect. We at Carleton—and I'm thinking of the faculty—have tended to become puritanical within our respective disciplines, even as the boundaries and character of these disciplines keep changing before our eyes. I'm speaking of English departments primarily, of course—for that's my discipline. English departments are in trouble right across the country, but they seem to me to be in more trouble at the good places than at the poor places. Our strengths are, as I say, becoming our weaknesses; in the pursuit of excellence we've managed to catch some of the lesser ways of being excellent—like being excellent literary critics about small lyric poems only, or excellent in the wrong century only—at the expense of keeping up with literature and language in the culture now. It's like being excellent on the moon. Our poets *and* teachers—some very good ones—keep cultivating moon excellence.

The solution is not clear. I offer another Shapiroism as a possibility (from *The Bourgeois Poet*):

Lower the standard: that's my motto. Somebody is always putting the food out of reach. We're tired of falling off ladders. Who says a child can't paint? A pro is somebody who does it for money. Lower the standards. Let's all play poetry. Down with ideals, flags, convention buttons, morals, the scrambled eggs on the admiral's hat. I'm talking sense. Lower the standards. Sabotage the stylistic approach. Let weeds grow in the subdivision. Putty up the incisions in the library facade, those names that frighten grade-school teachers, those names whose U's are cut like V's. Burn the Syntopticon and the Harvard Classics. Lower the standard on classics, battleships, Russian Ballet, national anthems (but they're low enough). Break through to the bottom. Be natural as an American abroad who knows no language, not even American. Keelhaul the poets in the vestry chairs. Renovate the Abbey of cold-storage dreamers. Get off the Culture Wagon. Learn how to walk the way you want. Slump your shoulders, stick your belly out, arms all over the table. How many generations will this take? Don't think about it, just make a start (You have made a start). Don't break anything you can step around, *but don't pick it up*. The law of gravity is the law of art. You first, poetry second, the good, the beautiful, the true come last. As the lad said: We must love one another or die.

I like that poem, if it's a poem, the way I like cigarettes: I know they're bad for me. Shapiro is telling us to head back to zero, and I've already come out against zero. But it's a Shapiroism, and I do think the possibility of moving back a couple of steps in our good colleges is very attractive. Maybe we don't have to *lower* the standards—I don't recommend that—just carefully neglect them in favor of education. We're really not doing very well at that, at education to the demands of the current culture; and I suspect the trouble is not just in English.

Which is enough for Yale and Yaddo.

X
xanadu

I could leave out "X," and nobody would mind. But there's Xanadu. "In Xanadu did Kublai Khan a stately pleasure dome decree." Xanadu gives me a chance to reject the word "romantic"—or rather to insist that it be let stand as a historical term beyond which poetry has moved. We obviously still have poems to which the label can be stuck, but I think most of them have a right to a new label. Charles Olson's label "projective verse" might do, but I suggest instead "theoretic verse." We have a good many kinds of the theoretic now, but let me stick to one kind and give a couple of illustrations of it. The first is an exercise of my own doing, maybe a parody of the kind:

> Like a clock I would wind her.
> Were I to mouth but the least immortal poesy, like
>   "Arizona has cool nights,"
> She would ogle, kiss, caress me into a deanship,
> And should I then shave, shower, dress, and neatly
>   descend to my orange juice,
> Her handbag would gush me *cartes blanches* and I
>   would, oh sweet thing,
> Despise myself for a cheat, me Keats, me Tarzan,
> For coming all over that sweetness, that child machine
> With Arizona.

You have the right to ask what that is about. I will tell you. It is about a poet prostituting himself; he is simultaneously bragging about his talents at prostitution and fearing, not very earnestly, for his poor prostitutional soul. The theme is easy and commonplace; the poem's excitement, if it has any, comes from the mishmash of odd, erotic details enforcing or illustrating the theme.

Here is a better example, the beginning of a fine poem
by Kenneth Koch called "Thank You":

O thank you for giving me the chance
Of being ship's doctor! I am sorry that I shall have to
    refuse—
But, you see, the most I know of medicine is orange
    flowers
Tilted in the evening light against a cashmere red
Inside which breasts invent the laws of light
And of night, where cashmere moors itself across the sea.
And thank you for giving me these quintuplets
To rear and make happy . . . My mind was on
    something else.

Thank you for giving me this battleship to wash,
But I have a rash on my hands and my eyes hurt,
And I know so little about cleaning a ship
That I should rather clean an island.
There one knows what one is about—sponge those
    palm trees, sweep up the sand a bit, polish those
    coconuts. . . .

Maybe the origins of this sort of thing are in the Homeric
listing. If you put a good Brooks-and-Warren analyst to
work on it he is apt to be a bit baffled—as Kenneth Koch
would like him to be—because the prose sense of the thing
—a mind turning down the opportunities of its world because the opportunities are all mad—comes to so little, and
because the detail is not the sort of functional stuff that
Brooks and Warren thrive on. The fancies sparkle a bit in
the sun, but they are idle, theoretical. To put it differently,
the feeling of the poem, and I think it has quite a bit, is
only indirectly and tenuously related to the "matter." The
matter consists of bundles of odd little mock-ups, like the
Tennessee in Wallace Stevens' anecdote about placing a
jar in Tennessee, or like the Arizona in my parody. The
mock-ups serve their purpose in their places, and then go
away.

In some respects these details are like the pleasure dome in Xanadu. "In Xanadu did Kublai Khan a pleasure dome *decree*"—that is, only khans, dreamers and theoretical poets can *decree* a pleasure dome; other people have to build them. I am also reminded of that marvelous structure in Milton's hell that rose like an exhalation. In all these cases the poets are of course dealing with imaginative experience rather than what we call real experience. I would distinguish radically, however, between the quality of Koch's imaginative experience and Coleridge's, or Milton's; for here is where it seems to me that Xanadu has changed. In Xanadu now, the poet is apt to be a dilettante; he doesn't really try to make the image "work"; he doesn't give us the whole scene as Coleridge did, with Alph the sacred river, and the caverns, and the walls, towers, gardens, and "oh, that deep romantic chasm which slanted/ Down the green hill athwart a cedarn cover." Instead he throws out an image and says, "You fill it in, you know it, you've seen it before," and concentrates instead on the brightnesses that will result from a variety of little rockets of detail all churning around.

I use the word "dilettante" to describe Kenneth Koch, a fatal word. Wallace Stevens is a greater poet than Koch, and greater than John Ashbery or Frank O'Hara or any of our other latter-day Xanaduists; and the theoretic quality of his verse is so individual that it is hard to think of him as fathering a school. But he did. If dilettantism is what we have, Stevens had a lot to do with it; for in his special way he has been our master theoretician. Not only did he deal with experience in the tentative manner I've described, but in most of his poems the theme of Xanadu—what Xanadu is, and what its relationships to experience are—appears constantly, with the pendulum swinging sometimes toward Xanadu, sometimes away, but always swinging sporadically, uncertainly, delicately, theoretically:

DISILLUSIONMENT OF TEN O'CLOCK

The houses are haunted
By white night-gowns.
None are green,
Or purple with green rings,
Or green with yellow rings,
Or yellow with blue rings,
None of them are strange,
With socks of lace
And beaded ceintures.
People are not going
To dream of baboons and periwinkles.
Only, here and there, an old sailor,
Drunk and asleep in his boots,
Catches tigers in red weather.

The nostalgia in that poem for the old sailor's drunken and inadequate Xanaduism is pervasive in Stevens; and sometimes, as not in "Disillusionment of Ten o'Clock," it wins out. One can adduce a biographical reason. For some poets, to be both an insurance man and a poet would be an occasion for "engagement." It was not for Stevens. He seems to have been a professional, though not a psychological, schizophrenic. He allowed little interaction to take place between his two "businesses," and as a result he has been much admired by the academic autotelicists I've inveighed against.

I'm unhappy that I admire him so much. As I've indicated, I'm not a purist, partly because I don't think a poet can achieve purity, and partly because I think he shouldn't if he could. So Stevens looks more and more like a villain to me, but a marvelous one.

The best way out of my value fix is to say that, though the danger is dilettantism, poetry itself is in some measure always dilettantism. It has always moved between Xanadu and Experience, and has therefore always been in this sense partially theoretic. The newness and wonder we keep expecting of poetry—and mostly not getting from it—will come, if it comes at all, from plugging away at the theoretic, the misty "X" even though the poets get called nasty names as a result, and though sometimes they deserve them. We must fear the "X," lest it turn us all into advocates of the old French witticism "And as for living, our servants will do that for us"; but we need it also. More of this later under "D" and Dolls, where I discuss Yeats. Yeats is a fine example of a poet who almost made it as a dilettante, then got off the train. Did Stevens ever get off the train? I'm sorry to say I doubt it.

W

war

"W" stands for War, the true antidote to Xanadu. So.
Once upon a time, back in the stone age of modern
poetry—that is, in the First World War—there was Wilfred
Owen. His most celebrated poem, *Dulce et Decorum Est*,
is a good place to begin any discussion of poetic rebellion or
alienation, since it attacks a prime social premise that has
been a pillar in the long-term coherence systems of Western
nations, the old Horatian platitude, "It is sweet and
honorable to die for one's country"; or perhaps, "It is
harmonious and fitting [or decorous or gracious] to die for
one's country." At any rate, "Dulce et Decorum est pro
patria mori." Here is what Owen said about the platitude.
He describes a gassed, dying soldier as follows:

> In all my dreams, before my helpless sight,
> He plunges at me, guttering, choking, drowning.
>
> If in some smothering dreams, you too could pace
> Behind that wagon that we flung him in,
> And watch the white eyes wilting in his face,
> His hanging face, like a devil's sick of sin,
> If you could hear, at every jolt, the blood
> Come gargling from the froth-corrupted lungs
> Bitten as the cud
> Of vile, incurable sores on innocent tongues,—
> My friend, you would not tell with such high zest
> To children ardent for some desperate glory,
> The old lie: Dulce et decorum est
> Pro patria mori.

I'm not going to analyze the poem—you can see that it's
inductive, experiential, though not cleanly so. Seeing is

believing. Horace, had he been around, might reasonably
have complained that he hadn't uttered the old lie at all,
hadn't said that a soldier's death is sweet and decorous—
death in itself is never sweet and decorous—but that the
ideal of carrying service to country to the extinction of self
is sweet and decorous. No matter—Owen won the day.
Compare his lines with these, written at about the same
time, but by a nonparticipant in London trying to describe
a soldier home from the wars:

> For he had faced the awful King
> Of shadows in the darksome Valley,
> And scorned the terrors of his sting
> In many a perilous storm and sally.
> Firm in the faith that never tires
> Or thinks that man is God-forsaken,
> From war's fierce seven-times-heated fires
> He had emerged unseared, unshaken.

I'll spare you more of that one. Maybe the author did meet
a soldier who had not been touched by war, but what war?
Not Owen's war. The awful capitalized King in this nonparticipant's Valley is an allegorical king out of a sermon;
so is the war storm, and so are the seven-times-heated fires
of the war.

Now here is another poem, a much worse poem by a
much better poet:

THE NEW MISTRESS

> 'Oh, sick I am to see you, will you never let me be?
> You may be good for something, but you are not good
>   for me.
> Oh, go where you are wanted, for you are not wanted
>   here.
> And that was all the farewell when I parted from my
>   dear.

'I will go where I am wanted, to a lady born and bred
Who will dress me free for nothing in a uniform of red;
She will not be sick to see me if I only keep it clean:
I will go where I am wanted for a soldier of the Queen.

'I will go where I am wanted, for the sergeant does not
    mind;
He may be sick to see me but he treats me very kind:
He gives me beer and breakfast and a ribbon for my
    cap,
And I never knew a sweetheart spend her money on a
    chap.

'I will go where I am wanted, where there's room for
    one or two,
And the men are none too many for the work there is
    to do;
Where the standing line wears thinner and the dropping
    dead lie thick;
And the enemies of England, they shall see me and
    be sick.'

[A. E. Housman]

If we look for the referents for these descriptions of war,
we find them not at the front at all, as were Owen's
referents, but where zero-hunters expect the referents for
old lies to be—in the dusty pious books that always buttress
the Establishment, in this case prewar books, books that
led country after country into the First War as if the war
were an Establishment picnic. Zero-hunters hate the Establishment, and they claim that to get out from under it, as
Owen did, and go out and look for the King in the darksome Valley on one's own is the first step to truth.

To believe in that first step—of looking—is to start on
the road to combating the Establishment, the prevailing
median; and most modern writers have shared with scientists a respect for at least this part of the inductive method.
When the poet looks at modern war the way Owen did at

the front, he will be hard put to write new national anthems.

But the looking process is not at root as clean and simple as it sometimes seems to be in the laboratory, or as it comes to appear to be in a simple, well-done descriptive poem. Even what we see is determined in part by what we have been educated to see; and what we select from what we see to put down on paper is a highly discriminatory act well beyond the perception act. Though the poet may decide on describing in detail a soldier dying in agony, rather than on composing a national anthem, he is engaged in constructing a poem, an artifice, just as is the anthem man. Prevailing social and aesthetic attitudes march in quickly to control or influence that construct. This is an obvious psychological fact that a poet shouldn't forget when he writes something that seems to him to be marvelously objective and realistic—yet he is apt to forget it. He will be prepared to acknowledge that all medieval literature was Christian, that Shakespeare was a slave of the royal Establishment, and that Dickens was merely a manifestation of the Corn Laws; yet on the question of influences upon his own work he is apt to be heard proclaiming that he writes as he pleases, describes what he sees when he chooses to see it, and is in general a free agent.

Let me give you a piece of another war poem to illustrate how different conditionings can produce quite different poems from rather similar war situations. This is a poem of the Second War by Shapiro:

> By chance I saw him die, stretched on the ground,
> A tattooed arm lifted to take the blood
> Of someone else sealed in a tin. I stood
> During the last delirium that stays
> The intelligence a tiny moment more,
> And then the strangulation, the last sound.
> The end was sudden, like a foolish play,
> A stupid fool slamming a foolish door,

The absurd catastrophe, half pre-arranged,
And all the decisive things still left to say. . . .

The situation in that poem is like the one in Owen's; and
for a reader interested in rough likenesses both poems will
do nicely as war-is-hell statements. With them we can
dash off a sociology book about the first part of the twen-
tieth century, observing that in both big wars the poet-
soldiers at the front discovered the "old lie." But rough
likenesses won't do for me here; the poems are saying sub-
stantially different things. Owen's soldier plunged at him,
got inside him, became part of his dream life. Reading the
poem, I got the sense that Owen lived that other's death.
Yet Shapiro's soldier was seen as an outsider, an alien,
described as like a character in a bad play whom the audience can't understand, much less identify with. To Shapiro
the pathos of the death (which he gets at more thoroughly
in later stanzas) was in its senselessness and remoteness.
To Owen the death was a horror because it was so close,
so relevant—to him.

  If our poets were all just reporters, the deaths they
report in the wars would be like auto deaths in the morning papers; we would note slight modifications in detail but
relentless uniformity of theme and effect. But poetry is not
essentially reportorial. Or editorial. It may report on a
scene thoroughly; it may argue an issue sensibly and well—
but it always does more than report and argue. The poet
can never detach himself from the sum of his own years
and causes.

  The sum of Owen's years and causes came to something that we see reflected in a good deal of the literature
of the First War. Owen did not discover the old lie; his
society did, and told him. So Owen was *ready* to write his
poem when the soldier plunged at him. Similarly Shapiro
had been told about the lie, and he was ready too—but

he had been told something else; the culture had whispered to him of the anonymity and loneliness of dying rather than of the blood and pain. Different wars, different sensibilities, but also different whisperings, leading to the selection, among other things, of different occasions to write about.

Poems, I am saying, sit around waiting for their poets to build them. The poet walks in his woods or his war until he runs into something that seems right. But why "right"? And how did it get that way? The rightness comes from the outside; then he seizes it for his own. Owen denied the lie, but he owned only a small piece of the denial. He was a soldier in a whole denial system.

In this connection let me mention two of my own war poems. I was in the service four years during the Second War, and in all of it I wrote only three or four short poems directly about the war. Not that I wrote much anyway, but I kept trying, and mostly what I came up with were literary things: observations about books I had been reading (I even wrote a sonnet about a First War book). Now, why didn't I seize my real opportunity? Why didn't I cope with *my* war?

I think my case was common in that war. The center of the war for me was administration and dullness. Dying soldiers were not plunging at me. I was stuck with tons of inanimate supplies, with paperwork, with lost trucks and gasolineless planes, not with death mostly. The few occasions I did seize were outside my humdrum war life, and they *were* about death—but death on the war's edges, for that's all I saw. Of the two I'll mention, one describes the grave of an American soldier, the other the grave of a German soldier. In both, the obsessive problem was, How does one *respond* to death? They were both written at the same time, the spring of 1943. They're both uneven and defective poems, I now think, but relevant here.

For their origins, imagine me steaming through the Kasserine Pass in North Africa alone in a jeep on a hot April or May day a couple of months after the last fighting there. I came across a number of temporary graves. I stopped and looked at them, ate my "C" rations. There was no other human being around. I went home, back to my outfit in Constantine, and wrote. Here is the first stanza of the American-soldier poem:

> Blatz was drafted, act of God and neighbors,
> For God and neighbors and the Better Life
> As Bangor, Boston, Bethlehem and Boise
> Live it. Blatz was drafted in the spring.
> By summer he had gone abroad to see
> What he could do. By winter he was buried.

In that stanza a denial system, a "no" system, is operating. All the patriotic jazz at home—the recruiting, the send-off, the basic training—leads very swiftly and senselessly to death in the desert. After the first stanza I develop the senselessness of it for two more stanzas, remarking on how brief was the interest at home in the death, and how in-auspicious a place a desert was for the attainment of military glory. Shades of Owen. But then what? Suddenly at the end, unlike Owen, I switch out of my "no" system and say,

> But in another country [that is, there by the soldier's
>   grave] strangers pause,
> Observing a special silence before his cross,
> Reading his name, poor Blatz, and possibly
> Dreaming of heroes.

The structure of the other poem, about the German, is different, but the burden is the same. In both poems I am terribly concerned with how I ought to feel (I ought to feel "no"), and at the same time I'm annoyed that anybody should tell me to feel that way. Both poems are heavily ironic. In the German poem I say that I should have no concern—that is, the system tells me I should have no concern—for a German death; but then I discover that I do have concern. I indulge myself in a little day-dream about the German's heroic and humane properties, and then I pretend to stiffen up and be soldierly again, ending with these ironic lines:

> And where he was born and moved with grace
> Through a pretty little pattern to this desert place
> Is no concern of mine.

That's enough of my youth. I bring it in here to display at a mundane level what seems to be a constant issue in the poetry of both wars, an issue having nothing to do with perceptual integrity, with denying old lies by looking the truth in the face. Is it not extraordinary that I, in the middle of a genuine, first-class wasteland, alone in a jeep, should be worrying about the proper *stance* or *manner* for me to adopt toward death? I might as well have been at home in a funeral parlor with all the relatives around.

A poem does get out of its Kasserine Pass eventually; it goes off in an envelope to be judged by somebody; hence its impulses and gropings are as much outward, toward an audience, as in the conventional public forms of rhetoric where audience is constantly acknowledged as a prime consideration. It does not matter that the envelope may never be opened; the audience or the image of an audience is something the poet carries with him when he writes the poem. That audience is part of what is sometimes nowadays called the Other. The Self has constant transactions with the Other even out in the Pass.

I'm going to get to Other, under "O" and "N" and other letters—it's a tough subject—but here under "W" the interest is in what some Other managed to say to all the lonely war poets in passes, producing at any given time a prevailing poetic norm. Were there such things as poetic norms for World Wars I and II? I think so. I think, for example, that the Owen poem is representative of the First World War in working toward a "rightness" of attitude that we find a whole group of poets sharing in that war, what I will call a "yes-no" pattern. The "yes" was in Horace's platitude, or some equivalent, and it came first; the "no" came later, out on the battlefield, unambiguous, sour. In contrast, the "right" pattern for Second World War poems seems to me to have been generally "no-yes," or, better, "no-maybe."

For unlike the First War, the Second War began with a "no," and part of that "no" was the "no" inherited from the First War poets, and from prose writers like Hemingway. Remember that we got into the Second War slowly; there was the Russo-German pact, the stagnant war in France, and then a whole series of deceptive, creeping involvements, especially for Americans, before we were thoroughly "in." Looking back on my own vacillations I can recall performing like a perfect Stalinist, switching from down-with-war on one spring day to beat-the-Nazis the next. Then came Pearl Harbor with its "yes," but even then we didn't have a missionary "yes." At best we thought, as we got shipped out, that we were getting on with the "yes," doing our job; at worst we thought we might get home safe. The original "no" had certainly been modified (few managed to stay wildly outraged by the Establishment) but our "yes" was a tiny "yes," for all the time we felt we were very small selves in a very big Other, and therefore resigned to ineffectiveness as no missionary is. If we were to find ourselves in the Other—that is, if we were to write poetry—we might do it, but only by getting off and away from the Other, as I thought I was doing out in the Pass.

So put in your notes that one war was a "yes-no" war,

the other a "no-yes" war. In the latter the "yes" came, if it came, tentatively, out on the war's edges, in scenes of soldiers in training, soldiers on furlough, soldiers swimming after battle, soldiers in bars—all removed from the hard military center as Owen's scenes were not—and dealing with death as a stranger, as Owen was not. The ending of the Shapiro poem I have already mentioned is just one example. It ends reflectively, on the edges, with a "maybe," with lines really remarkably like the lines I wrote about soldier Blatz in North Africa (Shapiro was out in the South Pacific). Shapiro's ending is an epitaph:

> Underneath this wooden cross there lies
> A Christian killed in battle. You who read
> Remember that this stranger died in pain;
> And passing here, if you can lift your eyes
> Upon a peace kept by a human creed,
> Know that one soldier has not died in vain.

I think Shapiro is saying that somehow the humanity of Christianity has survived this soldier's death, or perhaps been successfully defended by this soldier's death—so the death is not in vain. Similarly I think that in my Blatz poem the soldier's cross—though tentatively related to heroics rather than to Christ—suddenly blossoms into religiosity when the stranger (note that it is a stranger in both poems who experiences the sight of the cross) finds himself silently communing with the dead. If the war has brought about this communion, cultivating the Christian sense of charity and human brotherhood, then it has not been wholly futile, as it seemed it would be in 1939.

In Owen's poems what is asserted instead is that the war is an inhuman or dehumanizing experience, not the saving experience advertised in 1914.

I don't want to push my luck with these patterns, though I believe in them, loosely. I note for example a number of distinguished exceptions to the "no-maybe" pattern of the Second War. There's Henry Reed's "Naming of Parts," which is a "yes-no"; and then there is this short poem by Randall Jarrell, which seems to be "no-no":

DEATH OF THE BALL TURRET GUNNER

From my mother's sleep I fell into the State
And I hunched in its belly till my wet fur froze.
Six miles from earth, loosed from its dream of life,
I woke to the black flak and the nightmare fighters.
When I died they washed me out of the turret with
    a hose.

Do these exceptions to the patterns prove the patterns? No, but I think they *are* exceptions. The Second War produced a qualified and temporary but nonetheless genuine idealism in its participating poets generally, I think—until the Bomb.

Then the Bomb changed it all. Where are our war poets now? Or do we have any?

We have them, I think, but fortunately they're in Xanadu (not Kenneth Koch's, perhaps, but some other theoretical place, a place removed from the experience of war). They're marching in our pacifist army, and they're writing pacifist poems, anti-Bomb poems; and they're in Xanadu simply because they're not in the war. The Bomb has to drop, or the Vietnam War has to escalate to a point where it takes in the Owens and Shapiros, before the patterns I've been talking about will emerge. Until the War really comes, the big one, the poems being written will bear the same relationship to the experience of war as did the poem of the First War about the King of the darksome Valley.

Experience is hard to come by these days—this is one of poetry's troubles, one of the causes of Xanaduism in its many forms. So while we can be grateful for the absence of conditions capable of producing a new Wilfred Owen, we must, oddly, also be fearful of the paradoxical present remoteness of the violence and horror around us and ahead of us. I'm not sure poetry will survive, or the race will survive, our detachment from this violence, our TV-view or airplane-view of war. The detachment was moderately evident in "my" war, but now it seems built into war itself, for good.

The Pentagon and the White House are of course the places where the full implications of abstract, push-button killing need to be understood—what the poets think and say is a trifle here. Yet, since my subject is poets, let me suggest that we may have just run out of war poetry. We'll have Xanadu poetry, until a Tuesday. Then on a Wednesday we'll be dead.

Next time I'll move from Verse to Other.

2

FROM VERSE TO OTHER

V

verse

LAST TIME I talked about "closed verse" and "open-field verse," but I didn't get to the verse part. I was concerned with the modern artistic impulse to get out from under restrictions. I mentioned zero, I mentioned Wyoming—places for the poet to get out from under. I then denied the possibility of getting out from under. As illustration I made reference to certain thematic patterns that poets in two wars tended to observe even when they thought they were entirely removed from their culture—in the South Pacific or in the Kasserine Pass. I was trying to combat easy commonplaces about artistic freedom by reminding you that the lives of poets, like the lives of other men, are largely determined.

But under Xanadu I also described a kind of modern verse, which I called theoretic, in which, by the exercise of fancy, certain poets did in some measure manage to disengage themselves, though the disengagement seemed sometimes coy and artificial. I also noted a certain inevitable Xanaduism in contemporary war poetry and anti-Bomb poetry, which was a gesture toward disengagement yet also seemed to be controlled by the new sterile conditions of war. I have an anti-Bomb poem of my own in this genre, a characteristically modern, rebellious, anti-Establishment display of pacifism, which is of necessity removed from the experience it purports to describe and is therefore less experiential than fanciful. I pretend to refuse to dig a bombshelter in my backyard according to the prescriptions of civil-defense authorities. I compare such an act with digging a hole in my backyard as a child, and covering it with an old door and with dirt; then I conclude:

> But I'll not, no, not do it, not go back
> And lie there in that dark under the weight
> Of all that earth on that old door for my state.
> I know too much to think now that if I creep
> From the grown-ups' house to the child's house, I'll
>   keep.

Whatever the merits of my resolution there, the freedom I assume I have for digging or not digging is Xanaduish, that is, a bit unreal. Only when the sirens are ringing or the Bomb has dropped will I be able to say, experientially, that I won't retreat into childhood. I'm describing an ideal me there; the real me will come later, with the Bomb at hand.

I am not disrespectful of such poems, such resolutions. I'm simply trying to place them. I want you to understand that I'm not against freedom or against movements into open fields when and if there are any. I'm only against fervent rhetoric for freedoms and opennesses that do not exist, and against institutional encouragement of false expectations for freedom and disengagement in art.

Now verse itself. Verse has been that part of poetry most obviously closed, and so the battle for open-field poetry has frequently focused on verse. Many open-field poets would like to throw away verse but keep poetry. Not many Americans are well educated in the craft of verse, so throwing it away seems easy. It isn't easy. There's been a revolution in verse forms going on for about a century, yet half the verse being written is still iambic. Iambic forever. Or if it isn't iambic, it's another isochronic form; it's verse with the stressed syllables regularly spaced, verse making a noise, as Pound observed, like that of a metronome. The alternatives to isochronic verse are what we see in Whitman, Pound, the later Eliot, Williams and others. Most of these poets have been noted for their complaints about iambic, but they have made inroads upon such cadences only slowly. To me the stubborness of the old cadences, cadences rootedly opposed to the cadences of prose, is a clear indication of the strength of the forces opposing open-field composition. The truth would seem to be that the culture *wants* its poetry to be distinguishable from prose by its beat, and has therefore resisted attempts to diminish the distinction. It has felt that poetry somehow isn't poetry unless metronomic. It has wanted the tum-te-tum.

    This isn't to say that the culture is right. Ours is a prose culture, and for a prose culture to insist on the metronome is odd, maybe hypocritical. Maybe the culture wants its poetry clearly distinguishable from prose so that it won't have to take the poetry seriously. But whatever the reasons for the metronome's persistence, many a dissident poet who takes his work seriously, and thinks the world should take it seriously, is inclined to go against the culture's wish and eliminate the metronome or conceal it. He thinks of the poet's future as rhythmically in the realm of prose. This far have the rhythms of Shakespeare and Milton declined.

    The rhythmical properties of language are always obscure, difficult to pin down and talk about; but they're very important. Plato, speaking of the music of poetry, said that "any musical innovation is full of danger to the State and ought to be prohibited. . . . When modes of music change, the fundamental laws of the State change with them." Plato was an old Establishment man, but he was right. It is significant for the State and for the culture that we do now have a sizable force in poetry operating against the metronome, feeling its way around for "rightness" outside the old forms. Our musical condition is perhaps like that described by Matthew Arnold, with the old out of date and the new not yet born.

But that's not quite right. The new forms are here, but uncertainly. They have not been well articulated; one tends to have a feeling for them rather than a rationale about them. I know that personally I carry around with me—like old jazz tunes that one wakes up humming—a few cadences that tend to condition me in composing moments. Though my early work was heavily isochronic, the new tends to be offbeat or a mixture, a contrasting of regular and irregular passages. I've developed a real dislike of the number five—the pentameter part of iambic pentameter—so that when five shows up as the dominant line-unit force in something I'm doing, I get in there with cudgels right away and try, not very successfully, to beat it to death. Some of the rhythms that attract me now have been around for decades, but they seem very current to me; nor do I think I'm alone. A few examples:

Shades of Callímachus, Coan ghosts of Philetas,
It is in your grove I would walk,
I who come first from the clear font
Bringing the Grecian orgies into Italy, and the dance
     into Italy.
Who hath taught you so subtle a measure, in what
     hall have you heard it?
What foot beat out your time-bar, what water has
     mellowed your whistles?

Some would argue that Pound has not escaped the metronome here, for he has a pretty regular two-stress line unit going even though the quantities of unstressed or partially stressed syllables vary. I won't argue. For me the distinction of the lines is not so much in the stress pattern as in the pause, or rest, pattern. English poetry has not been noted for its silences, that is, for the *control* of silences,

breaths. It has been chatter chatter chatter right on through
—with a few songs for exceptions. In these lines Pound has
complete control of the rests, as if there were in the background a musical instrument playing, filling in when the
voice stops.

  Another, very different example:

How nice it is to be superior!
Because, really, it's no use pretending, one is superior,
    isn't one?
I mean people like you and me.

Quite! I quite agree.
The trouble is, everybody thinks they're just as superior
    as we are; just as superior—

That's what's so boring! people are so boring.
But they can't really think it, do you think?
At bottom they must know we are really superior
    don't you think?
don't you think, *really*, they *know* we're their
    superiors?—

I couldn't say.
I've never got to the bottom of superiority.
I should like to.

This little D. H. Lawrence thing has none of the aspira-
tions, musically, of the Pound piece. All his life Pound has
been working on a new music for poetry, whereas Lawrence's musical ambitions were slight. But Lawrence's
casualness and deliberate inartistry I find very suggestive;
he manages to shift the musical issue completely away
from stresses, and all that—stress problems as they arise foot
by foot—to the larger, looser stress factors tending to gov-
ern the music of prose. Lawrence is making poetry of banal
conversation; Pound is up in the heavens writing sym-
phonies. I find both ventures attractive.

  Let me conclude here with a couple of examples out of

my own recent work, one prosaic and staccato, the other conventionally metronomic. The first is the beginning of a poem not yet finished—God writing in his diary:

Dear Diary:

At last.
I'm back.
I sit down again at this dusty desk,
And start to write in these pages,
And feel like a stranger.

The trip was exhausting. Endless committee work, wrangling, touring the danger spots.
I hate to live for centuries out of a suitcase.
I hate provincial legislators, hate petitions, hate formal dinner, hate simpering small-talk with small-time satellite bureaucrats.
Touring out there I had a big fantasy life going: the wonders of home.
Now, ten minutes home, the fantasy's gone, I've a terrible migraine
From just sitting in my old lab with my old scope, looking.

The second illustration is the introduction to a long poem of mine, "The Seven Days":

On the last day of the old world I stretched
Out my bones like a fossil fathoms down
And bade time's leavings cover me layer on layer
And death sweep over, over me in her sea gown.

On the first day of the new world I stood
On a porch on a hill in the dark with a pencil
And bade there be light in the east and took my pencil
With me into the light and set to brood.

So much then for Verse, at least until I get to "M" and Music.

U
unity

I hate "U." "U" is Unity. I'm going to fly right on by it to show I'm still free. Which leads to "T."

T
talent

"T" could be Tradition or Talent or Technique or Tactics or Theoretical—I've already mentioned Theoretical—or Togetherness or Tone or Trope or Troubador. "T" is big. It's hard to get past "T." I'll take "Talent," but only briefly, worrying the problem of the relationship between Talent and Energy. "Energy" is a big poetic word these days; it tends to supersede "Talent." Throughout the tirades of most modern rebels against conventional forms it is implicit that the traditionalist poets of our time (who usually get called "academic" poets) lack energy. Not that a respect for energy is new. Think of Browning's poor old Andrea del Sarto, so accomplished, so talented, and so dull. Think of Edgar Lee Masters' "Petit the Poet" who, surrounded by "tragedy, comedy, valor, and truth, / Courage, constancy, heroism, failure," kept struggling with his little verse forms:

> Triolets, villanelles, rondels, rondeaus,
> Seeds in a dry pod, tick, tick, tick,
> Tick, tick, tick, what little iambics,
> While Homer roared in the pines.

Whitman may have begun the rage for the word "energy"; at the beginning of *Song of Myself* he says:

> I, now thirty-seven years old in perfect health begin,
> Hoping to cease not until death.
> Creeds and schools in abeyance,
> Retiring back a while sufficed at what they are, but
>   never forgotten,
> I harbor for good or bad, I permit to speak at every
>   hazard,
> Nature without check with original energy.

Later he sounds his "barbaric yawp over the roofs of the world." Pretty good, that yawp—one can't deny it. I remember trying to, when I was younger. Some editor friends and I printed in our magazine a chaste obituary announcement, decorously surrounded by black, announcing "to certain of our unprinted contributors the death of Walt Whitman." We were wrong; he's still around.

But a yawp is still not the same as talent. A puppy can yawp, and so can bad poets, many of whom think that poetry is a simple act of energy transference from glands to speech. Unfortunately, in our age the craftsman demands of the art have been so upset by constant innovations in the craft that old procedures for teaching the craft and assessing competence in it are upset. As a result the myth persists that energy—what football coaches call desire—is all that matters. And with the decline of conventional standards for assessing the simplest craft talents in an art, the myth makes some, though not much, sense. Every man a poet. Don't worry about talent. Just yawp.

S

scene

Which leads to "S" and Scene. Let's say that the scene is my desk. I'm sitting at it. I see something, hear something, read something, feel something. The desk is the scene for it all. Or, let's say that the scene is political. I immerse myself in *that* scene, have feelings about it, act in it. Two different kinds of scene: one local, one general; one physical, one conceptual. A distinction of Kenneth Burke's.

Problems of scene get complicated, but I want to be simple. Going back again to the Stone Age of modern poetry, we see that part of its original impulse derived from a contempt for what some nineteenth-century poets had been doing with scene. When Arthur Hugh Clough said, "Say not the struggle naught availeth," where *was* he? Pound and Ford Madox Ford wanted no more of that; they urged both poets and novelists to go back to the rendering of specific scenes and actions—hardly a new thought, but one that had gotten lost. They wanted to start with local, sensed details and move out from there to concepts or even leave the concepts out entirely. Call it an inductive art they recommended, an art on location.

Here is Pound ridiculing the mistiness of scenes and acts of love as he saw them in magazine verse before the First World War:

1. Spring is a pleasant season. The flowers, etc. etc. sprout, bloom, etc.
2. Young man's fancy. Lightly, heavily, gaily, etc. etc.
3. Love, a delightsome tickling. Indefinable, etc.
   A) By day, etc. etc. etc.
   B) By night, etc. etc. etc.
4. Trees, hills, etc., are by a provident nature arranged diversely, in diverse places.
5. Winds, clouds, rains, etc. flop through and over 'em

Pound was not trying to distinguish between real and imaginary scenes, but between the concrete and the fuzzy, the particular and the general, the clearly sensed and the vaguely felt. Like Wilfred Owen, he would have nothing to do with sceneless platitudes. In the scenes of war or any other kind of human experience lay the truth of experience.

Owen, of course, became so thoroughly committed to the war scene in France that he became literally a one-scene man for his short poetic life, a regionalist of the trenches. In this respect he may be compared with a number of conventional regionalists, all one-scene men primarily: Frost with his half-real, half-mythical pastoral New Hampshire and Vermont, Ransom with his patrician South, Robinson with his Tilbury Town, Masters with his graveyard. The one-scene poet is in the great tradition of scene; scene is his "Establishment," or part of it, and even if he does not trouble to sketch in more than a fragment of the total scene in any one poem, still the sense of the whole is there, reinforcing the fragment. He knows where he *is*, a point regionalist writers love to make when opposing the delocalized shenanigans of nonregionalists. The southern novelist Andrew Lytle once said of some southern hill people, who were said to think New York lay to the south of Tennessee: "It was the tragedy of these people that they ever learned where New York lay, for such knowledge has taken them from a place where they knew little geography but knew it well, to places where they see much and know nothing."

But the return to specificity of scene in the early part of the century characterized the work of nonregionalists as well. Eliot, Pound, MacLeish, Stevens, Auden—all of these men were scene setters, none really regionalists. For them a scene had a different function. It was not background; it was not the land on which the poem was built; the "real" scene for them was that second kind of Burke's, a general conceptual scene of which specific concrete scenes were merely instances.

Now to think in these general terms about scene is to move sharply away from traditional scene setting. If we look for an explanation of why modern poets like Frost and Robinson look so different from modern poets like Eliot and Pound, we can hardly do better than note that Eliot and Pound lacked a local sense. They were multiscene men in life and in art. They were not physically gummed down to a piece of Tennessee, and they were not persuaded that they could do what they wanted in their art if they gummed the art down. They felt that a one-scene operation could not reflect the big world of which they felt themselves a part. So, though sharing with the regionalists a respect for the concrete, they wanted to play tricks on the concrete.

Both Pound's *Cantos* and Eliot's *The Waste Land* are big exercises in comparative scene setting. Scenes become, like characters, agents of the action rather than the under-pinnings for the action. We get little tidbits of local scene, but they merely add up to general scene. The general scene is the Waste Land, or the world.

Archibald MacLeish has been multiscene too, but he has tended to take one scene a poem. He has been all over—inside circus tents, aboard planets going out of orbit, with Cortez in Mexico, on a beach in the sun, and so on.

Cummings was also a one-poem one-scene man, but he liked to take a fragment, some special property of the scene, and fiddle with it; and as he grew older his tendency was to move away quickly from the scene he may originally have visualized to some quality of the scene, generally abstract ("anyone lived in a pretty how town").

Stevens roamed everywhere. He gave us seascapes and landscapes; he gave us scenes of Florida, Tennessee, Min-nesota, Connecticut, half the other states; he gave us still

lifes inside and outside, by day and by night. But his impulse was not so much to render a scene as suggest it, toy
with it, conjure up some banal essence of it, and then
leave it. In a characteristic Stevens theoretical scene he
tells us that "Boston should be in the Keys" and "Charles-
ton should be New York." As for Auden, he has gone
in for scene setting in earnest in his latest book, traveling
through his Austrian house and writing poems room by
room. But he will not be remembered chiefly for this kind
of scening; his interest has been in composite scenes; he
has been a sort of sociologist of scene in poetry.

What I am getting at is that the primary movement in
modern poetry has been away from regionalism, from fixed-
scene, one-scene work. The uneasy alliance between the
regionalists and the other advocates of the concrete has
tended to obscure this movement, but it is there.

It is the bad part of the move from regionalism that
keeps being called to our attention, the part Andrew Lytle
observed in his hill people, who were taken away from the
little that they knew well to the much that they didn't
know at all. Certainly all modern men, poets or not, tend
to get a very eccentric vision of reality from looking constantly at a collective scene, a hypothetical scene, a national or international scene, a sociological scene. Between
the sociological scene and the mundane but special farm-
yard, the mind has to make so many difficult adjustments
that it sometimes feels lucky to come out sane. For the
sense of place is close to the sense of self. If we lose the
local sense, the sense of place, we are apt to lose also the
impulse to write poetry, which is among other things a
continuing investigation of the *where* of self.

This is why I began talking about scene in terms of me
at my desk. I have a number of poems that begin there.
Sometimes I feel that the desk is the only solid scene I have
in my deregionalized world, the world I keep trying to
deal with in my poetry. The desk is the only thing I have

with roots. This is a momentary fallacy—I know better—
I know that my life is crammed with local scene—but I
know also that these localisms have tremendous competi-
tion now from the general, the collective, the abstract; so
the fallacy has some basis. It is a depressing fallacy, and
very modern.

R
roots

Which leads to "R" and Roots. Almost interchangeable with scene. I said that Eliot was not a one-scene man in his poetry, not a regionalist, not a man of roots. But he always approved roots. Coming from a rootless country, he wanted a country with roots (and he got one). He thought, "No roots, no culture." He had a friendly English rival, Wyndham Lewis, with lots of roots, who professed to hate roots. They were always arguing. Lewis thought America's rootlessness marvelous. He described America as a "great promiscuous grave" into which would tumble "all that was formerly race, class or nationhood." When that happened we would all be there in its "wholly excellent vacuum."

As I see it, the virtues and vices of roots have been talked to death, while the roots, for better or worse, have tended to thin out. This is why Whitman remains so modern. A century ago Whitman was a vacuum poet after Lewis' heart. He denied regions; he embraced the world. His scene was either the self or the world, and he tended to make the self scene and the world scene the same. He listed dozens of other selves out there in the great Other beyond the self—duck-shooter, pilot, carpenter, lunatic, printer, half-breed, squaw, connoisseur, and so on—he listed them, and then said:

> And these tend inward to me, and I tend outward to
> them,
> And such as it is to be of these more or less I am,
> And of these one and all I weave the song of myself.

Whitman is with us now in Allen Ginsberg's "Howl,"

for example—Ginsberg himself makes the acknowledg-
ments. He is with us in most poems about the atomic
bomb, where the self's problems and humanity's problems tend to become indistinguishable; and certainly with
us in the new Pop Poetry that Bob Dylan's work may be
taken as an instance of. He is also with us, I'd say, in the
guise of most of our current college students. There's a
great big "we" floating around now, a vacuum "we" that
is built deep into the pacifist movement and the integration movement and the student rebellion movement; and
this "we" is a delocalized, conceptual, transcendent, Whitmanian "we" that hundreds of thousands of little selves
are caught up with.

Though it seems futile to go about being nostalgic for
roots that one doesn't have, like Miniver Cheevy, it seems
futile and also hypocritical to deny roots one does have.
Each of us has a name, a race, a past, a local being that
constitutes a good bit of our essence, our truth. And though
we may not be happy about that essence, we are sure to be
lesser poets, and maybe lesser men, if we deny it and think
of ourselves only collectively as manifestations of some big
invisible lump. That new millionaire Bob Dylan would
have been wise to remember his true name and heritage—
not indulge himself so with the vacuum myth—when he
wrote in one of his ballads that his name and age meant
nothing. Obviously they have meant a great deal to him
both economically and poetically. This is enough about
roots. I'll be back to Bob Dylan later, under Guitar.

Q
quest

Let me be abrupt for a few letters. "Q" is for Quest, of course. According to Northrop Frye, all literary genres have a quest motif built into them. This proposition seems less profound if one adds that all human actions have a quest motif built into them. Questing is part of our continuing transaction with the Other, and it may involve chasing the Grail or satisfying a "neural itch."

A good bit of modern literature seems to go at its questing negatively; that is, it opposes questing, recommends sitting on the back stoop. I've already complained against the quest for zero, and will soon be complaining about the quest for the Absolute; but I'm hardly against questing. Questing presumably enters this discourse under every letter—like "P," for example.

P
piety

"P" is for Piety. The central piety of poetry is a faith that it has occult powers. The sum of its parts does not account for the whole. When its raids on the inarticulate succeed, we would like to know why and how, so we disarticulate it, and lo! we are back with the inarticulate again. Magic?

Some of this is just trade piety. We real insiders can rhyme not only "moon" and "spoon" but "face" and "lice." We can yoke together unyokables like lovers and parallel lines. We can load a rock or birch tree with holy significance by our technical dance around it. Magic?

Anyway, what has the dance to do with the rock's or the tree's holiness? Was it not holy before the dance? Is not the world charged with the grandeur of God before the poet gets to work on it?

These are questions without clear answers. The poet answers them by asserting his faith in the transaction between poet and rock. The poet starts the transaction (because of his neural itch). He supplies the word, and magically the word turns out to be God's word. The word then sits between them—his and God's word—common property—theirs.

But I really don't need to bring God in here. Take two familiar secular poems, William Carlos Williams' "Red Wheelbarrow" and Robert Frost's "Mending Wall."

> So much depends
> Upon a red wheelbarrow
> Glazed with rainwater
> Beside the white
> Chickens.

and

> Something there is that doesn't love a wall,
> That sends the frozen ground-swell under it . . .

These are hardly religious statements in a conventional sense, but they do insist upon mystery. Both of them have an unexplained entity that the poets make a good deal of not explaining (Williams' "so much," Frost's "something"). Williams doesn't touch his "so much" with a ten-foot pole. Frost goes into his "something" a bit; to his ignorant neighbor he describes the "something" as elves—but that's a joke; he withdraws it and supplies no other explanation.

But Frost does say—and I think Williams implies—that although the something is ineffable it is not unknowable. Who knows it? The poet. Who doesn't know it? In Frost's poem the old stone savage next door doesn't know it. He is the antipoet whose path to knowing is obstructed by his blind acceptance of a social platitude, "good fences make good neighbors." In Williams' poem we are not told who the antipoet is, but we can imagine. It's anyone who can't understand the poem, can't sense the importance of the transaction between poet and wheelbarrow.

The poet's role is obscure and changeable in such transactions. In the wheelbarrow and wall poems he seems to be largely a sensitive receiving and transcribing apparatus. In others he appears more positively as the initiator, even the maker of the transaction (many poems by Yeats are like this, especially "The Tower"). There's a whole spectrum of transactional situations in poetry, but in all of them the transaction is hopefully more than a prose transaction, something beyond the literal, the sum-uppable; it is what is called (by Philip Wheelwright) translogical.

In the modern push to make poetry concrete and specific, a very characteristic stance is Williams': the poet looking at a thing, meditating upon it, drawing something out of it. Call this descriptive poetry, or poetry of observation. To the novice it seems *merely* descriptive. He is a student in a creative writing class perhaps, and he is asked to develop his perceptive powers by playing at being a painter, by painting the wheelbarrow in words. So he misses the part about the "so much" or the "something." He thinks of the exercise as only an exercise, and he dreams of the day when, after finishing his apprenticeship, he can get poetic. He doesn't know that his teacher has religious designs upon him, is asking him to see God or the Other right there and then in the wheelbarrow or wall.

This is enough on Piety, except for one other example of the "magic" of the "translogical" in a contemporary poem (I'm trying to give you a small anthology as I go along). It is a poem by James Wright that carries on as a characteristic poem of simple observation until the very end, when Wright translates observation into "something" or "so much" else:

Lying in a Hammock at William Duffy's Farm in
Pine Island, Minnesota

Over my head, I see the bronze butterfly,
Asleep on the black trunk,
Blowing like a leaf in green shadow.
Down the ravine behind the empty house,
The cowbells follow one another
Into the distances of the afternoon.
To my right,
In a field of sunlight between two pines,
The droppings of last year's horses
Blaze into golden stones.
I lean back, as the evening darkens and comes on.
A chicken-hawk floats over, looking for home.
I have wasted my life.

O
other

I've already mentioned Other, and will do so again and again. I could summarize everything I've been saying under Other.

Poetry is a continuing transaction between Self and Other.

A poem is a Self-Other—that is, a Self that has gone out and made it, momentarily, with the Other.

The poet moves toward zero to flee some false Other, find some true Other.

He goes to Yale or Yaddo that he may be put in cahoots with the Other.

He tries out Xanadu as his own perfect Other.

He experiments with verse as a mechanical Other that will help him to the "real" Other.

He knows that his talent will eventually be measured by the Other.

He knows that scene is where the Other lives, and that roots are what the Other used to provide.

He goes on quests for the Other.

He displays piety in his search for the Other, by not naming it.

And always the Other remains tricky and evasive. If the poet catches it he catches it only obscurely and in poems. The critic catches it not at all but talks interminably about it, mostly by breaking it up, dissecting it, looking at it piece by piece. At least so the anticritics say. The critics are the *bad* Other, say the anticritics. G-rrrr.

Next time I'll begin by taking the piece of the Other we call Nature, Nature being "N." As preface to that, let me leave you here with a poem by Howard Nemerov, to which I'll refer:

A Spell Before Winter

After the red leaf and the gold have gone,
Brought down by the wind, then by hammering rain
Bruised and discolored, when October's flame
Goes blue to guttering in the cusp, this land
Sinks deeper into silence, darker into shade.
There is a knowledge in the look of things,
The old hills hunch before the north wind blows.

Now I can see certain simplicities
In the darkening rust and tarnish of the time,
And say over the certain simplicities,
The running water and the standing stone,
The yellow haze of the willow and the black
Smoke of the elm, the silver, silent light
Where suddenly, readying toward nightfall,
The sumac's candelabrum darkly flames.
And I speak to you now with the land's voice,
It is the cold, wild land that says to you
A knowledge glimmers in the sleep of things:
The old hills hunch before the north wind blows.

3

FROM NATURE TO
GUITAR

N
nature

LAST TIME I concluded with a poem by Howard Nemerov called "A Spell Before Winter." In it Nemerov was describing a Vermont landscape. I read it because it's a nature poem, and I wanted you to think about nature as a manifestation of the Other. Vermont is a fine manifestation of the Other, but so are Wisconsin and Minnesota. They are crammed full of nature, and I like them: the long contours of the hills, the air's clarity. You won't find me knocking nature, east or west. But I'm not going to be sentimental about it either, and tell you how close I am to nature. I'm a city poet, and I've only rarely felt that trees and hills were profitable objects for me to conduct my poetic transactions with. Mostly, as I say in one poem, I feel like a fool out there with the birds. I commune with the famous line by Wordsworth, "Little we see in Nature that is ours," but for the wrong reasons.

It isn't that city life has deprived me of nature—Northfield, Minnesota, where I live, is hardly *deep* city—but that it has given me what seem to me adequate substitutes—people instead of birds, books instead of talking brooks, and so on. My affection for birds and brooks is great, but I have never assumed that I could contribute much as a poet to their presence. Accordingly I have tended to work a bit diffidently on the edges of nature—somewhere near the town line. Here's an early antinature piece of mine, called "God's Acres" (I owned six acres in Connecticut once, which some friends and I christened "Wise Acres"—the usual cute suburban business—but we never hung up a sign):

> He who can tell a grosbeak from a grackle,
> Red oak from maple, marigold from heather,
> May get on. But will that other,
> Inward drawn,
> Who never on his T-shirt smugly
> Sewed at camp a badge or feather
> For mastery of wood or shore or meadow?
>
> Not likely.
>
> His is not a placid, plotted
> Nature trail of brae and coot,
> Dingle, willet, plash and pintail,
> Botany and fruit,
>
> But thorns, thorns, thorns, his flesh to scratch
> As he slogs nameless in his briar patch.

But I'm not unconditionally anti-Wordsworth in spirit. I frequently wish (despite an anti-Wordsworth poem I'll put here in a footnote*) for a friendlier Other, a warmer

---

*WORDSWORTH AND THE WOMAN

> ". . . travelling southward from our
>   pastoral hills,
> I heard, and for the first time in my life
> The voice of woman utter blasphemy . . .
> I shuddered . . ."
>   *The Prelude*, Book VII

Old shuddering Wordsworth, I'm in your country.
I've got rocks, trees, little hedgerows, and a big sky

nature than a brambles nature, a nature filled with all the
spirits Wordsworth found there. In other words, I like
nature, and wish in weaker moments to be a scoutmaster;
I only draw the line and beg off on mergers, permanent
mergers with nature. I'm with D. H. Lawrence on this. Nature is the Other; it is not the Self. It is in fact the Self's
opposite, the unSelf, the phenomenon *out there* that remains inaccessible to the Self so long as the Self *is*. How, I
say to myself, could it be other than good that nature remain inaccessible, remote, not quite communicable-with,
so long as the Self is? I think its inaccessibility is good. I
prize the distinctiveness of Self from nature simply because I prize the distinctiveness of Self itself, what there
is of it, a Self that I know is partly hemmed in by nature,
a Self that I've been preaching the *great* limitations of, a
Self with nature as a dark, uncontrollable conditioner. I
want the Self distinct, not merged—to the degree that it
can achieve distinction. I want it to have transactions, yes,
but not merger. You can go on living after a transaction.

Under which I too can be solemn, godly, portentous
When I'm angry. You make me angry.
I read you beside a simple pastoral fire
A hundred and sixty years after you shuddered,
And I say that by god an honest woman or man
Who'd fit god's scheme
Has a duty to blaspheme.

For when I see what an honest woman or man
Puts up with in the name of god and the son
And the holy ghost and a thousand other pieties,
Including those of yours out in the hedgerows,
I don't even need to think that god gives a damn
To know that if he has pleasures he'd have pleasure
In seeing you shudder.

An honest woman or man has a moral duty,
Man, to use god's name in vain when the establishments
Which put his name on their doors are vain,
Including that temple of rocks and fastidious naturals
Of yours, man.
So, from the other ranks,
I send to the girl who defiled that temple: thanks.

Remember Wordsworth's poor old girl Lucy. She was the one who, when dead, rolled round in earth's diurnal course with rocks and stones and trees. I'll hold off on that as long as I can. The day of true oneness with nature is the day of death.

But transactions are another matter. Any poem or prayer is created on the assumption that the Other is not *wholly* alien, inaccessible. Any poem or prayer is a movement out toward it, a tentative gesture but a gesture. The poem reports the gesture, the transaction makes the Other seem to respond for a moment, seem accessible.

I made it seem accessible to my youngest child a few years back, when he was getting his first bedtime stories. I was a big smashing success with a story about Jimmy Skunk. Having been brought up on Thornton W. Burgess, I knew my way around in nature in Burgess' way, and the beginning of my story, which came to have dozens of variations, was essentially this: "Once upon a time Jimmy Skunk was going lippety lop, lippety lop down the road for his breakfast, when suddenly out of the bushes a big bad dog came barking out at him. Jimmy Skunk was very frightened and he didn't know *what* to do until he remembered his smell bag." Well, it goes on from there. My son has gone on from there now too. Instead of a smell bag, now he wants his heroes to defend themselves with guns, hand grenades and planes. He's becoming a big militarist. My point is that the story was a success because I supplied the Other out there with the ingredients it needed to be attractive to the boy. He could identify with Jimmy Skunk. He did.

So as poets, as makers, we make the Other accessible by a trick—sometimes known as the pathetic fallacy—and if it were only a trick poets might well remain Thornton W. Burgesses and Walt Disneys forever. In fact, some of them do—they are taken in by their own trick; they supply the Other with what they would like the Other to have, and they look at it with great pleasure. I remind you of the story of Narcissus.

But where the tricks leave off and the truths begin is a matter for the best philosophers. In the Nemerov poem I read you, the poet announced that he was speaking to us with the land's voice. A trick?

Let me get at that question by going back briefly to an earlier nature in poetry, the nature of the old pastorals. It is convenient to think of the pastoral tradition as ending with Gray's "An Elegy in a Country Churchyard." Poor Gray. His poem is a fine poem, and it shouldn't be blamed for Rousseau, Wordsworth, the French Revolution, and Marx—but it was written at a strategic time, and therefore frequently appears as the villain. It represents both a political and a literary view of nature that passed out of style in the eighteenth century; and because it passed out of style its trickiness is out in the open; that is, the poet's tricks in appropriating nature now seem more obvious to us than they would have seemed to those brought up in the old pastoral tradition.

Literarily the poem gives us a prescriptive vision of nature. As many critics have observed, it is a bundle of literary commonplaces about nature—that is, commonplaces in the old sense, rhetorical commonplaces, what Aristotle called *topoi*. It was William Empson who noted that these literary commonplaces also had political overtones. He took these lines:

> Full many a gem of purest ray serene
> The dark, unfathomed caves of ocean bear;
> Full many a flower is born to blush unseen
> And waste its sweetness on the desert air.

Not only, he observed, was the nature being described here an idyllic literary nature (think of shepherds and philosopher sheep in the background), but it was a Tory nature. Politically the lines favor the *status quo*: "a gem does not mind being in a cave, and a flower prefers not to be picked; we feel that man is like the flower . . . and this tricks us into feeling that he is better off without opportunities. . . . We ought to accept the injustice of society as we do the inevitability of death."

Now, when we get to Wordsworth a few years later, nature, far from buttressing the going political establishment, is vaguely subversive. We see little in nature that is ours because we have given our hearts away to a bad system. If we could retrieve our hearts we would find that nature provides a fine alternative to the system.

I'll leave you to decide whether nature is going republican or democratic in our time—but, when you work on deciding, I suggest that you forget the farm vote. From the beginning the pastoral has really been a city form—that is, not written by rural swains for their sheep, but by city people for city audiences—so it has taken its prescriptions from the city. It still does. When Nemerov, a New Yorker who graduated from Harvard and served in the Royal Canadian Air Force, says that he speaks to us now with the land's voice I'm inclined to believe the land had some help.

Oddly, I find Nemerov's nature a bit closer to Gray than to Wordsworth, at least politically:

> I speak to you now with the land's voice,
> It is the cold, wild land that says to you
> A knowledge glimmers in the sleep of things:
> The old hills hunch *before* the north wind blows.
>   [my italics]

It is a more unfriendly nature than Gray's, but its "knowledge" is rather similar; it "knows" that all things come to an end, that the movement is down and away, that there is no resisting, and that you as a hill or a man can only hunch up a bit—or maybe turn up your coat collar—to protect yourself temporarily from the blast. I'd be inclined to call this Tory "knowledge"—but I would add that it also seems to me to be true. I find his transaction with the hills a trick, but a reasonably honest trick; I can see those hills and imagine them saying that to *me*. There's honesty for you.

As poets we are probably less prescriptive about nature now than we used to be. We're leery of the pathetic fallacy; we tend to be inductive in our preliminary approaches to nature, and to describe the scene as reporters before attributing qualities to the scene. We also have a whole genre of what I will call the antipastoral. *The Waste Land* is an example; so is Auden's elegy to Yeats. In both these poems the old pastoral commonplaces of a sympathetic nature filled with human feelings are referred to, but ironically. Thus in old elegies nature had drooping willows in it, and daffodils filled with tears. But in Auden's poem, by deliberate contrast, nature has gotten hard-boiled:

> He disappeared in the dead of winter:
> The brooks were frozen, the airports almost deserted,
> And snow disfigured the public statues;
> The mercury sank in the mouth of the dying day.
> O all the *instruments* agree [my italics]
> The day of his death was a dark cold day.

It seems clear that in an antipastoral like this, and also in a fairly inductive experiential poem like Nemerov's, the poets are more impressed by the objectivity or essential Otherness of nature than Gray ever was. Little they see in nature that is theirs. Or less they see there than Gray did. Wordsworth's observation has become a commonplace; we acknowledge it as a permanent fact about the condition of modern man, not as a new and shocking condition that ought to be remedied.

I ask only where that non-Gray fact came from. Did

the birds and the trees provide the fact? Answer: Obviously the fact is a man-fact. When an Auden or a Nemerov conducts a transaction with a bird or a tree, the bird or tree is a passive partner. The bird or tree doesn't like being cheated, but doesn't say anything. Not only does Auden or Nemerov initiate and control the transaction, but he looks for approval of the transaction less to the bird or tree than to a third party, an audience. For a poetic transaction is never completed (as I said under War) without reference to an audience, a potentially *listening* Other. Birds and trees are nonlistening Others. Poems have never gone over well with birds and trees.

Inevitably a transaction with bird or tree will be aimed in part at some audience's vision, some audience's prescriptions for bird or tree—just as in Gray's case. The difference between Gray and Auden is largely a difference in audiences. Auden's audience is prescribing a nature that is not his; Gray's was not. Or, to put it differently, Nature is still getting her fashion news from the city, just as she used to. What she should wear and how she should look are prescribed by the culture now just as in the old pastorals. In this sense our nature poetry hasn't changed, and won't.

M
music

The composer Elliott Carter was at Carleton recently on a lecture program rather like this one. His description of the differences between the old and the new musics effectively persuaded most of us there from the other arts that all the arts have been party to the same revolution, the revolution from closed forms to open-field forms. He pointed out that some of the new music has a comparative culture base like the poetry of Eliot and Pound; and some of it has tried to go directly to nature in the inductive manner I've been talking about; for example, it has gone to the woods and brought back on tape the real sounds of eccentric birds. And some of it has been marked by violent rhythmic and harmonic changes, arrived at with or without the help of computers. In these experiments the composers, like the poets, have been asking themselves what the possibilities are in their art if the artist starts all over, from zero. It seemed to me, as I listened to Carter, that composers had a clear advantage over poets in their zero-hunting because they were not tied down, if they chose not to be, by anything with roots to it like the common language, but could simply use the full range of the computer in programming combinations. Yet the more I listened to Carter, the less sure I was that this theoretical advantage amounted to much in practice, since the payoff in music as in poetry was made finally by the human Other I've mentioned, the third party. The Other's readiness for particular innovations—rather than the computer's readiness—would, it seemed to me, finally decide on the validity of the innovations; and the Other's presence would be sensed by the composer even as he planned programs for his computer.

Of course, it must be acknowledged that up close the

Other—which in this case is nothing but the Culture itself, or a piece of it—looks like a moron, and not many artists like to be caught catering to its fickle tastes. Its vacillations seem to be largely determined by the popular press and by publicity schemes—a difficulty I'll discuss under "F." But at a distance the Other has a stable look, a look of knowing better than it knows. It is not worth listening to on anything contemporary, but in the long run it is a stable judge, a Solomon—at least this is an article of artistic faith.

What I am getting at is that the Solomon side of the culture as audience and arbiter is obscurely tied to music, the music of language. I am back with Plato, you see, who warned against changes in the music of poetry because he felt they affected the stability of the State itself. But I'm not concerned here with the State. I'm saying that at the heart of any value system for poetry must be some musical norm for language, a norm subject to change but changeable in an evolutionary way, not changeable overnight by promoters with novelties. One simply can't dismiss the historical evidence tending to demonstrate musical stability in language. It would seem that the culture has some monotonously persistent rhythms and harmonies in its subconscious, and that the sensitive artist can catch these harmonies and thereby distinguish himself from the insensitive artist or entrepreneur artist or computer.

And if the poet *can* catch them, the culture will listen to them, and keep on listening even after the critics have all gone under the sea—this is another article of poetic faith.

This subconscious, underground music must be partly determined by our unchanging physiological patterns, and their relationships with days, nights, tides, moons, seasons— this has been called the "existential base" (Erich Fromm). But it comes as well from the life of each generation as it passes. That is the temporal underground (Fromm calls it the "historical base"), an underground not of the moment but still fleeting, an underground motion slow enough to make the music of Whitman sound modern, but not slow enough to do the same for Pope. To sense that temporal music, and somehow to put it together with the deeper, more permanent human music, is the task of every poet—in the Kasserine, in Vermont, in Greenwich Village— and it is a task at which he always feels alone. Perhaps computers could help him here; perhaps they could assess the rhythms of common speech, and the rhythms of various deviations from the common, and come up with what our administrators call "guidelines."

But I doubt it. I don't know how to deal with music, or talk about it, and I therefore suspect that a computer will not know either. Music is built in deep, way below the textbooks on prosody, way below the expertise on the music of poetry. It is not just rhythm, for example—and I want to get off rhythm because I've already dealt with that under Verse. The old forms or genres of literature—like comedy, tragedy, elegy, sonnet, whatnot—can also be thought of in musical terms if we are willing to think of music as harmony and coherence as well as rhythm.

When Aristotle blocked out tragedy for us, he was proposing a closed musical arrangement. He went through the various fixed elements in the form and then described at length the action, or movement itself, in all its prescriptive intricacy. And where are his prescriptions now, and the other closed-field forms? I'd say they had been as much upset by the new open-field world in which literature finds itself as have the old rhythmical patterns like iambic.

T. S. Eliot's musical career suggests what has been happening. His progression from "Prufrock" through "The Waste Land" to the *Four Quartets* makes a good case study of how a sophisticated poet-musician, finding himself in what looks like an open field, works himself slowly back into a closed one, but a closed one of a different kind from those he rebelled against in the beginning. I have already described "The Waste Land" as antipastoral; I would also describe it as antinarrative (in passing let me add that it is also anticharacter). With reference to narrative, in both "Prufrock" and "The Waste Land," but more so in the latter, we find the old quest motif at work: Prufrock sets out in his mind for the parlor he never reaches (we can even spot the point in the poem where he abandons the quest, and begins to talk in the past tense about what he *might have done*); the Waste Land figures dimly reenact the Grail quest, but get practically nowhere. That is, in both poems the narrative quest pattern keeps being disrupted. So the basic movement is out and away from the old pattern, which won't do, to something new, something that never quite takes shape in these poems. It's a "things-fall-apart" development, and any musician could provide modern equivalents for it in music, perhaps starting with Charles Ives.

Then with the *Four Quartets* Eliot, having given up the narrative pattern entirely, and having picked up a good bit of training in the juxtaposing of disparate themes, scenes, and impulses along the way, suddenly composes four quartets. Literally quartets. I can't pretend to parse them as a musician might; I don't know what parts to assign to flute and oboe, what to violin, what to brass; nor could I mark for you where the various themes separate or come together, for they always seem to be overlapping, fusing. But I can assert that each of the quartets is a quartet in the sense that it takes four themes and works them around and around. The four themes (the same in all the quartets) are past, present, future and the oneness of them all.

As a hopefully relevant aside, let me quote Freud:

The activity of fantasy in the mind is linked up with some *current* impression, occasioned by some event *in the present*, which has the power to arouse an intense desire. From there it wanders *back* to the memory of an *early* experience, generally belonging to infancy, in which this wish was fulfilled. Then it creates for itself a situation which is to emerge *in the future*, representing fulfillment of the wish—this is the daydream or fantasy, which now carries in it traces both of the occasion which engendered it and of some past memory. So *past, present* and *future* are threaded, as it were, on the string of the wish that *runs through them all.* [My italics]

So there's the threading of the *Four Quartets* in a nutshell. Freud is of the opinion that past, present, and future are somehow threaded on the strings of all poems. This may be so, but no other poem I know deals with the threadings so explicitly as the *Four Quartets.*

What interests me about the Freud comment is that with it one can see, at least speculatively, the jump that Eliot had to make to get away from the old narrative music and start fresh. The jump is from the frame of action *in* time, which he has already sensed as inadequate, into the fantasy life where time is fluid and subject to arrangement.

So with the *Four Quartets* we have on our hands a musical innovation of some consequence, but I suspect it is of consequence because the third party—the Other, the audience—has a fantasy life too, according to Freud's prescription, and also a subterranean feeling for the intertwining of musical themes à la J. S. Bach. That is, the audience doesn't come to it cold at all, as well it might come to an "arbitrary" poem or sonata built by a computer. Though an innovation in verse, the form will seem quite natural because it is an old form in music—and also in our fantasy life.

The *Four Quartets* is among the few musical successes we can boast of in modern poetry; and though I've been going on too long about music I would not be doing justice to the subject if I didn't mention failures. Not many modern poets have had the musical acuity of Eliot, and I think there's a good literary reason. Most of us have been conditioned to think of our musical problems visually. Absurd maybe, but true.

Obviously the basic problems in music are problems in sound and time that can't be caught on a printed page. As a poet, one has to *listen* to other poets, and to read one's own work aloud to many kinds of audiences, before one can really begin to think of poetry in solidly musical terms. Yet poetry readings as a whole are a degenerate form (some of them are good, but collectively they drive people out of auditoriums in droves), and the cause of their low state is not to be found in the paucity of great reading voices like Dylan Thomas'. I'd be inclined to blame instead Brooks and Warren—that is, the New Criticism. I was brought up under the sway of the New Criticism, and while what I learned from it may have been beneficial in many ways, I think it probably set back my musical career about twenty years.

For a number of good reasons, mostly pedagogical, the New Criticism taught us to *look* at poetry harder than poetry has ever been *looked* at before. It told us to look at a poem not once but many times, and to see its images, its verbal and syntactical emanations, its ironies. It even taught us to think of problems of tone and rhythm visually. Rhythm in Brooks and Warren is a bunch of daggers and half-moons over printed words; tone is an attitude or stance rather than a quality or sound. I will grant important connections between these visual matters and musical matters; I'm not underestimating the values of a visual approach. But the trouble with visualizing the poems constantly has been that we've stopped hearing them. The poet growing up to the demands of the New Criticism is oriented to the eye rather than to the ear. I go through some mystic rites, for example, connected with writing lines in longhand first, and then typing them, all the time feeling that until the whole work is typed clean it is not done. Some people might therefore describe me as anal; I prefer to think I'm

Brooks and Warrensy. If I had been brought up in an oral and aural tradition, I would presumably have wanted to hear my poems on tape before pronouncing them done; but I'm insensitive to tape. This is partly me, of course, but Brooks and Warren played a big part.

One of the most unmusical characteristics of typographic poetry, I think, is its compression. I was amused to hear Elliott Carter observe of some recent electronic music that its rhythmical variations were so complex and delicate that even his trained ear could not detect many of them; he had to read the program notes to find out what was happening. The same trouble is to be found in poetry, and it is especially noticeable at poetry readings of compressed, typographical poems. A listener just doesn't receive all the wonderful innuendoes in tone and rhythm that the poet laboriously built in. That is, he doesn't get them until he does a Brooks-and-Warren on them. The eye can go over and over the printed page, but the ear is allowed just one hearing before the poet runs off to the next small liberal arts college. Oral effects have to be sterner somehow, and certainly of longer duration, to do their work. Many short lyrics read in auditoriums are over before their audiences know they've begun. If the poet is going to perform complicated musical gyrations, his model should be something like the *Four Quartets* rather than haiku.

Of course, a guitar would help. I'll get to guitar. But a change in the poems themselves would help more. I have nothing against good typographical poetry, but I think that in the search for the underground stability for musical values in language the ear needs to be educated, the eye stabled. So I see some virtue in the revolt of the fifties against academic poetry; at least it took poetry out of the books for a bit and put it into noisy bars.

A little poem by Jack Gilbert should be included here. It is called "Orpheus in Greenwich Village," and though it's a typographical poem it makes a good point:

What if Orpheus, confident in the hard-found mastery,
should go down into Hell?
Out of the clean light down?
And then, surrounded
By the closing beasts
And readying his lyre,
should notice, suddenly,
they had no ears?

Now I have to have a crash program for getting through a
few letters that could be important but will have to wait
for some other spokesman than me.

L
love

"L" is for love. What else? I remember somebody writing a learned review for a magazine I edited saying that no good love poems were being written any more. But only the other day my ten-year-old son, who has been listening to Beatle records for a quarter of his life, rushed up to his mother with one of the records and said angrily, "You know, Mom, these are all *love* songs." Love is the sweetest thing. Love is a mess like Christmas. Cummings is a great love poet. There are no islands any more. We must love one another or die. All poets are lovers. I refuse to worry about love, except when it's abstract. Enough of Love.

K
kulch

"K" is of course for Kulch, a subject that would give me a chance to talk about Washington and the new arts program, and festivals on the White House lawn. Things I got involved in last year. But I've talked so much about that elsewhere that I don't want to. Kulch is what we get when we are terribly earnest about art and think it should uplift us. It has been the big bourgeois impulse to Kulch that has put our artists on pot in blue jeans in cellars. On to "J."

J
jargon and jingles

I don't like J.

I
images

My text for "Images" is from Allen Ginsberg, the opening lines of a poem called "A Supermarket in California":

> What thoughts I have of you tonight, Walt Whitman, for I walked down the sidestreets under the trees with a headache self-conscious looking at the full moon.
>
> In my hungry fatigue, and shopping for images, I went into the neon fruit supermarket, dreaming of your enumerations!
>
> What peaches and what penumbras! Whole families shopping at night! Aisles full of husbands! Wives in the avocados, babies in the tomatoes . . .

Then having made his bow to Whitman, Ginsberg goes on to distinguish between what Whitman was able to do in the supermarkets of his time and what a poet does there now:

> Where are we going, Walt Whitman? The doors close in an hour. Which way does your beard point tonight?
>
> (I touch your book and dream of our odyssey in the supermarket and feel absurd).
>
> Will we walk all night through solitary streets? . . .
>
> Will we stroll dreaming of the lost America? . . .
>
> Ah, dear father, graybeard, lonely old courage teacher, what America did you have when Charon quit poling his ferry and you got out on a smoking bank and stood watching the boat disappear on the black waters of Lethe?

I choose to interpret the end of this poem (it's a nice poem, and a good introduction to Ginsberg's big supermarket poem, *Howl*) as saying that America is now hell. Hell has its supermarkets too, and the poets in it can still choose between the avocado counter and the apple counter, the trouble being that the avocadoes will now turn out to be poisoned, the apples made out of plastic.

I'd say that most of our younger poets—that is, younger than me—have been getting their images from some Whitmanian supermarket in the last few years. To construct a poem of any length the poet gets together a hundred dollars' worth of merchandise from all over the store, then combines it eccentrically, as Ginsberg did—babies in the tomatoes, and so on. Compare this procedure with that in an old-fashioned image-evoking poem, Robert Frost's "After Apple Picking." When Frost went to the fruit supermarket, he went for apples and the essence of apples or the idea of apples—and that's all. Apples were plenty for one poem. Save the avocadoes for the avocado poem. He was confident that if he really worked on apples, and put them in a significant human context, he would have a poem about more than apples. He had faith in the ultimate breadth of the narrow vision.

Remember what I said about "scene." I am saying the same thing now about "image." The supermarket poet flits from place to place and image to image; he can't spend ten seconds with apples. His development principle is to extend and include rather than to select, concentrate, refine. As Ginsberg said, he produces enumerations in the Whitman manner, great listings. A poem is more a collection than an ordering—not great riches in a little room, but many bright fragments in a whirlwind.

H
happening

I would have you think of happenings of two kinds, public and private. Normally the word is applied to public happenings only; so when we hear the word we are apt to think of dramatic performances without a script. In such performances the participants try obscurely not to order experience but to let experience order them—and to do this in front of an audience that will be alternately miffed by players who haven't learned their lines, and charmed by the spontaneity of it all.

Poetry readings are about the only place where the happening principle can be exploited, publicly, by poets. I have never dared to improvise a poem on the spot on a stage—or perhaps I should say that I've never had enough presence of mind to do so—but I've conducted enough poetry readings to have a feel for the art, and I'm thoroughly persuaded that it is a happening art. You have to go into it feeling irresponsible but eloquent, which is to say that you have to have a few drinks first. Our occupational hazard. And you have to draw the audience in on the happening by hook or crook. (Katherine Ann Porter is reported to drop her gloves; I tend to stutter appealingly and look helpless.) Yet all this time you have a thoroughly prepared script or set of scripts to which you must adhere like glue; so the happening part of the program is severely limited.

The larger happening in poetry is the private happening. We have had a version of this for decades: what is called automatic writing. Psychologists like automatic-writing games in verse; so do mathematicians and amateur poets, maybe because the games allow them to indulge their conviction that anybody, or any machine, can write the

kind of poetry that is being writ. It is a mark of the confusion in poetry that the popularity of automatic writing
as a device for being creative goes along side by side with
the continuing push for a highly disciplined poetry. The
perfect modern poem would incorporate this contradiction.
It would be an instant villanelle. Still, automatic writing
has not achieved the status of serious art in most circles;
it is not the basic happening for poetry.

The basic happening, also a private happening, is
simply the poet at his desk trying not to be automatic,
trying to *control* the creation of a new world—the image
with which I began these lectures. He is there empty but
expectant, starting his first line or image or Homeric simile.
It's a moment of uncertainty and cigarettes and coffee and
vague itchings. The mind is hopefully clear and the pencils
are sharp, but the paper is white. There's an impulse to
create, but little, apparently, else. Certainly the control of
the impulse has not yet appeared; and though the plan for
the poem may already have been programmed in the mind
of God, God hasn't told the poet yet. The poet therefore
feels free, and as the poem grows the mystery of how it has
grown remains part of the fascination of "creation" for him.
He thinks he is creating, controlling the growing, but he
isn't sure.

Robert Frost once interestingly described how he grew
out of the free happening condition in which he began
"Stopping by Woods" to a condition where he found himself thoroughly programmed by his own earlier decisions:
In the first line he was free. Then he was stuck with iambic,
then to a stanza form with three rhymed lines and one
"free" line. The free line, however, became in turn a commitment for the second stanza, which then proceeded to
give birth to a "free" line committing the third stanza.
This pattern was satisfactory until Frost decided he wanted
to stop, at which point he discovered that he was programmed to go on forever (the free line prescribing endless

additional stanzas). So his next assignment was to break out of his own commitments without being a traitor to them, that is, to unprogram himself. This he did by the trick we all know, of simply making the free third line in the last stanza rhyme with the others, that is, by repeating the "miles to go before I sleep" line.

Pretty good happening, I'd say. Also an interesting account of the verse-programming process. But it is deceptive. It suggests that the programming for the poem was largely a matter of settling on the rhyme, and then of being run by it. A mathematician reading the account might conclude that he could have programmed the same poem for production by a computer merely by taking these factors into account. That is, he could have removed the problem from the mind of Frost and turned it over to the machine to *happen*, as soon as the preliminary conditions of rhyme (meter being given) had been agreed upon.

This deceptive simplicity was inadvertent, surely. Frost was not one to aid and abet poetic happenings in computers. Poets are uniformly leery of computers for a variety of reasons, most of which are contained in a fine essay by Howard Nemerov called "Speculative Equations." They want to feel as free as a computer to try infinite combinations within neatly prescribed patterns, but they also like to imagine that they are choosing the patterns, are not automatic, are not (except in rare instances like *Kubla Khan*) being happened to. It is on this point that they split sharply away from the linguists and the psychologists of language, who like to imagine that eventually scientists will be able to describe (and therefore control) all the complexities of the process of verbal happenings, even verbal happenings of a high order, like poems. Poets are shocked by such a possibility—shocked by the possibility, that is, of the control moving out of their hands—and so they are seldom to be caught giving scientists clues to the process, as Frost did unwittingly in the remarks I mentioned above.

The whole modern ideological split between scientists and poets lurks here, and as Nemerov points out in his essay, neither the poets nor the scientists seem to know quite what they are arguing about.

On the one hand the scientists—at least the behaviorist kind—imagine that eventually any creative process of the mind will be understood as a learning or growth process like any other, and understood in sufficient detail to be replicable. For them the happening principle in art is simply a version of the random activity at which computers have been in other fields demonstrably superior to man; so they think that as soon as they know enough of the components of a poem to be able to feed the computer a decent diet of experiential stimuli, the computer will outdo the poet in responding to that diet.

On the other hand the poets, while possibly acknowledging that the creation of a poem is analogous to other "growths" in the mind, tend to be merely insulted by the notion that a scientist or a computer will ever be able to understand or evaluate the components of such growth. If artistic growth is a happening, and a partly programmed happening at that, still it's a mysterious happening, hence not machinable.

Both sides seem to be wrong. Scientists can make incredibly simple or stupid remarks about the learning or growth process with an air of having just discovered something marvelous,* while poets can deny the immense orderly machinery that has traditionally been a part of language and verse, simply to insist upon mystery. If the two sides would only speak to each other once in a while we might eventually find out what a happening is. Until

---

*Here are a couple of instances from Jerome Bruner's recent book *Toward a Theory of Instruction*. First: "The ability of problem solvers [for my purposes here, read "poets"] to use information correctively is known to vary as a function of their internal state"; and second: "Teaching is vastly facilitated by the medium of language. . . ."

then I will subside on happenings by simply reading the beginning of a pleasant poem, *Circus of the Sun,* by Robert Lax,
about a major happening. The poem is atavistic in insisting
upon the ancient mysteries of analogy, and therefore characteristic of poetic refusal to acknowledge what has been
going on in the lab all these years; but it is nonetheless an
eloquent description of that basic happening, the beginning
of a world or a poem. It is probably *as* sufficient a description as we shall have for some time to come:

Have you seen my circus
 Have you known such a thing?

Did you get up in the early morning and see the wagons
    pull into town?
Did you see them occupy the field?
Were you there when it was set up?

Did you see the cook-house set up in the dark by lantern
    light?
Did you see them build the fire and sit around it
    smoking and talking quietly?
As the first rays of dawn came, did you see them roll in
    the blankets and go to sleep?
A little sleep until time came to
Unroll the canvas, raise the tent,
Draw and carry the water for the men and animals;
Were you there when the animals came forth,
The great lumbering elephants to drag the poles
And unroll the canvas?

Were you there when we stretched out the line,
When we rolled out the sky,
When we set up the firmament?
Were you there when the morning stars
Sang together
And all the sons of God shouted for joy?

G
guitar

Orpheus had a lyre. Bob Dylan has a guitar. Lyres are out, guitars in. My daughter has a guitar, my oldest son a four-string banjo, my youngest son a plastic ukelele. I'm too old to know what this means, and I'm not sure that it has anything to do with poetry; but to the extent that poetry is something to be sung I'd guess that the transition from lyre through lute and virginal to guitar signifies poetry's descent from heaven to earth, from a thing of the gods to a thing of plain, humble, simple hill folk like my twelve-year-old daughter.

I've already mentioned the big collective "we" of which Bob Dylan and many other folk singers sing. I don't know if I have really expressed my doubts about that "we," particularly my doubts about the traditional artistry of the "we." Anyway, this is no place for a history of folk songs. I merely take the familiar scholarly line about them that no well-known folk songs have been composed spontaneously by unlettered hillbillies at hoedowns. The tradition of the ballad, for example, like the pastoral tradition, has been a relatively sophisticated one, and the composers of most well-known ballads seem to have been minstrels (or whatever) of considerable technical accomplishments. They have been literary folk, artists. Yet they have obviously operated on a social and artistic wavelength way down the dial from the "serious" poets. They have been aggressively lowbrow for centuries, and still are. They have adopted rustic or proletarian ways. They have cultivated unlettered speech. They have gathered around them listeners and critics who disapprove of an intellectual approach to art and who talk disgustedly of how the "serious" poets fail to reach the people, fail to come to grips with basic humanity, and are precious, high falutin, arty.

Unquestionably theirs *is* a different circuit, economically and artistically. And though in our melting-pot America we are always being confronted with odd crossovers, there seems little chance right now of the circuits combining.

I think we "serious" poets could learn quite a bit from the likes of Bob Dylan, but I'm not persuaded we are any artier or more precious than he is. He has a good many strings to his guitar. Coming from the depressed iron-range country of Minnesota, he sounds (or at least used to sound) like a socialist out of the thirties as he describes miners and other economic derelicts caught in the machinery of a bad capitalist system. And coming from our new, guitar-playing generation he also makes the proposed revolution a revolution of youth against age, telling us in a ballad that mothers and fathers shouldn't criticize what they don't understand and should get out of the way of the new generation.

His songs *try* to be strong stuff. They seem to demolish our society as they go twanging along. If we were to take them at face value, the HUAC would be after him in a minute.

But somewhere along the line he stops being an energetic activist and becomes just an exile with a guitar, an exile in fancy—planning to leave tomorrow; could leave today; just a pawn in the game; a rollin' stone; and so on. He is alone and yet surrounded, if we believe him, by a whole generation of pawns, rollin' stones. This is the "we." It all loves guitars and roads, but it has no political solidarity, no social solidarity. That side is negative, a socialism manqué.

I'm hard on Dylan, but I do think something is missing in this oddly uncollective collective effort that he in a way represents (though perhaps he has now been too successful to continue to represent it properly). I picture a revolution of guitar players, hundreds of them. The revolution as show biz. There's something unreal about it, an unrealness accentuated in Dylan's case (and many others) by his adopting old folk song ways in front of a Greenwich Village backdrop. Dylan senses the difficulty. Sometimes he takes his hillbilly role seriously; sometimes he's strictly tin-pan alley (the department of that now known as folk-rock), and sometimes he's intellectually quite pretentious. But he's made a profession out of zero-hunting, and he's stuck with it. To put it differently, he has adopted a child's role, so that when he wants to talk grown-up matters (which, to his credit, is frequently), he has to lisp them out in childish numbers.

Listening to him, I am reminded of a Jules Feiffer cartoon where a father is talking to his grown-up son and complaining that the son simply won't *be* grown up, preferring childishness. The son replies (I paraphrase) that with adults acting the way they do, it's better to remain childish. I can sympathize with the son's position. We adults have little to recommend us. Nor do we "serious" poets have much. If a child could lead us, I for one might follow. But—and this is the catch—Bob Dylan is not a child, not a hillbilly, not even a simple dedicated revolutionary out of a mine shaft. Nor are his audiences of college students children. Playing at child when one is not a child is a deception; it destroys the whole point in the argument for being a child, the old Wordsworthian point that children are not as deceived as men are.

So my last word on Bob Dylan is not "basic" or "proletarian" or "real" or even "cool," but "baroque." Is that a dirty word? I don't know, but I'll leave you with it. Next time come "F," the Absolute—and of course Curtains.

4

FROM F —— TO THE
ABSOLUTE

preface

I CAN'T summarize the previous lectures, but I might spend
a minute reminding you how I have traveled backward
through the alphabet from "Z" to "G." I talked of modern
zero-hunting, or primitivism, and pointed to the impossibility of achieving zero. I mentioned Yale and Yaddo as
instances of benevolent institutions that encouraged artists
in their cultivation of a separatist, unengaged, near-zero art
(here I found both the artists and the Establishments in
error). I brought in Xanadu and its recent equivalents:
what I called "theoretic" poetry. I talked interminably
about War, and patterns in war poetry that tended to
suggest engagement in the most extravagantly unengaged
situations. I talked about Verse patterns, and how difficult
it was to escape them, suggesting some recent noncon-
formist patterns. I did nothing about Unity. I said Talent
and Energy were not the same. I talked about Scene and
Roots together, pointing to the abandonment, in much
modern poetry, of single-scene poems, perhaps as a consequence of our troubles with Roots. What did I do with
"Q"—Quest? I did nothing with it. I mentioned the Pieties
of poetry, and I prattled constantly of the Other. I did
Nature in, pointing out that nature in poetry was always
as much a manifestation of the poet as of the great green
wonders. Music, then, I discussed, mumbling about the

81

Four Quartets. Kulch I slid over, and Love, and Jargon; then touched Imagery briefly, especially supermarket Imagery. Then there were Happenings, which I didn't say all I wanted to about, and Guitar, which I said more than I knew about.

Now here we are. Surely I said more than this?

F ———

"F" stands for all four-letter words, and for Fraud.

A recent Supreme Court decision against the publisher of the magazine *Eros* introduced a question related to the issue of obscenity that booksellers and deans and literary critics and even the American common man have been talking about for a long time. For introducing the question the Court has been roundly d*mned. The Court, said its critics, remuddied waters that had at great labor been cleared. Their decision was a legal disaster. The country would now be inundated with new attempts at book censorship from militant agencies of decorum.

The question the Court raised (and then came up with an answer: No) was whether pornography was properly a sales gimmick. Now, what is so novel about this question? I can think of no previous Court decisions that have dealt with obscenity plain; always some other question like this one has been attached. The judges have consistently looked for something to redeem the obscenity in the work being judged, some indication of "serious artistic purpose," some trivial trace of social, cultural, or moral concern. In other words, they have always said that obscenity needs to be redeemed. Furthermore, in looking for possibilities of redemption, they have always by implication been confronted with the opposite: the possibility that it is unredeemable. But what is the unredeemable? The unredeemable, as they seem to see it, is simply a book whose obscenities are primarily present to lure buyers, a book that uses obscenity as a sales gimmick. Hence I don't see that the judges have been inconsistent in their new decision. For decades they have tried to judge books in their social, moral and artistic context, and in doing so have consistently

fenced in the abstract issue of freedom. Freedom has always been fenced in thus by courts.

So much for the Court's inconsistency—they have not
been inconsistent. But is the Court right? Should the
freedom of the artist be tied to the ethics and conventions
of the society—business ethics, sexual ethics, any ethics?
For a long time our artists have mostly said No, and nowhere have their demands for an "open field" been louder
and shriller than on the subject of dirty words. The society's
traditional prudishness about dirty words has been a focal
point for artistic rebellion, so that many artists have rushed
into obscenity not for some serious, redeeming artistic
purpose, but simply to defy the society, and demonstrate
their liberation from it. They have come to see decency,
always a lesser virtue, as a major contemporary vice, and
have felt pure and missionary in fighting it.

But now that obscenity has been demonstrated to be
a surefire way, maybe the only surefire way, to sell a book,
the purity of the obscene has also become suspect. A few
literary careers and a number of publishing empires have
been built on obscenity, and they have unsettled the whole
structure of trade-book publishing, hurtling a number of
hustler artists into the uneasy role of entrepreneur. To
the writer genuinely offended by the intrusions of com-
merce upon art, and by sensationalism as a way to literary
grace, some of the legal issues the Supreme Court has been
wrestling with all these years begin to look like artistic issues
too.

I can't imagine that any artistic reaction to obscenity
would go so far as to become an artistic movement in favor
of censorship. On censorship no modern artist can be expected to see eye to eye with the judges. But I can imagine
that some writers, who under less favorable "sales" cir-
cumstances would have become "authentic obscenicists"
(Karl Shapiro's phrase), might now, in reaction against the

gross and corrupt commercialism of obscenity, go all-over
Victorian and chaste in their writings. No, not quite.

I remember some words on this by a philosopher, Peter
Caws, at a meeting at the Library of Congress last year.
The dirty-word issue had erupted there in a gathering of
little-magazine editors, and the great old dome of the
Library had been rocking slightly, when Mr. Caws pointed
out that four-letter words had been traditionally the property of the working classes, most of whom were thoroughly
conditioned to restrictions upon their use and were therefore much more shocked by their public use or literary use
than were the sophisticated bourgeoisie. To the extent,
therefore, that the literary men demonstrated their freedom
by using these words in public situations, they identified
themselves with the bourgeoisie—that is, the villain class,
the class cause of corruption—which was a poor way to
start a revolution.

I have oversimplified Mr. Caws' remarks—he did qualify them, noting the fuzziness of these old class terms now
—but I like the direction of his remarks anyway, because
it leads us away from that old hat, freedom. I've been talking incessantly in these lectures about the limits of freedom, and will continue to do so. In the matter of four-
letter words, or of obscenities in general, it seems to me
that the artist's problem with them, as distinguished from
the judge's problem, is of finding and asserting his own
Voice as he uses them, a Voice that is not something he
can turn on and off like a phonograph. A personal illustration: I was in the Army four years, and I know that my
vocabulary was somewhat modified by it (the Army was a
long course in vocabulary enrichment). Yet even four years
of unceasing verbal obscenity didn't persuade me that my
Voice—you know, the nice, sweet, decorous, bourgeois Yale
Voice of the son of a doctor brought up on a nice street in
a nice neighborhood in a nice college town—ought to be

or in fact could be essentially an Army Voice. So while I'm really quite beyond being shocked by obscenity, just as a large part of our educated bourgeois class is beyond being shocked (but as the Army still is not), I'm persuaded that my motives would not be sound artistic motives if I were to sit down now and write a book to be censored in Boston. The Voice of that book, for better or worse, would be false to me as an artist. It is on these grounds that I would condemn the book, though I wouldn't censor it.

The spirit of rebellion, and the resultant drive for some sort of liberation that has characterized so much of modern literature, has effected great changes in our literature and life, changes I can see and tick off in my own short thirty literary years—so you won't catch me denying the revolutionary forces in the neighborhood. But to be always leading the revolution (to be, that is, in the terms of this discussion, always in the avant-garde in the use of certain words or in the description of certain privacies—note how chaste I am being—to which the Establishment takes exception), to be always out there in front waving the banners of new freedoms from old nonsense is a role that the artist can play only at the risk of failing to accept another obligation he has to his artistry, the obligation to see and account for himself as he is, not as he thinks he ought to be. He may believe the society's prudishness is profoundly wrong, but as a product of that society he necessarily partakes of that prudishness—he is part prude himself—so he is merely living a fantasy life, a theoretic life, an oddly moral rather than existential life, if he writes poems or stories that remorselessly conjure up for us an emancipated artist, nude, on pot, in a house of what used to be called ill-repute. I have nothing more to say on this depressing and boring subject.

E
the expressive, and epiphany

"E" is for the Expressive, and for Epiphany. I will be staccato. The Expressive appears as the rival of the Literal. Read Philip Wheelwright's *The Burning Fountain*. The Literal gives us a language of clear entities and clear distinctions. It provides rational procedures for focus, for elimination of irrelevancy, for progression, for exposition. The Expressive works outside the prescriptions and the clarities of the Literal. It entertains contradiction, paradox, meanings with "soft focus," meanings partly determined by tone, meanings with "significant mystery." Maybe the chief difference between poetry and prose will come to be the difference between the Expressive and the Literal; though for this to happen, much that is now prose would have to be called poetry.

I talked about the Expressive two sessions ago, under "Piety." (Remember "The Red Wheelbarrow.") Really, the piety of poetry is faith in the Expressive, or alternatively a lack of faith in the sufficiency of the Literal.

Denise Levertov has written a poem describing the Expressive. It is called "The Third Dimension." In it she says in effect that the third dimension, though it is the one that takes the other two dimensions out of geometry and makes them real, is the dimension you can't see. She says:

> . . . Honesty
>
> isn't so simple:
> a simple honesty is
>
> nothing but a lie.
> Don't the trees

> hide the wind between
> their leaves and
>
> speak in whispers?
> The third dimension
>
> hides itself. . . .

She goes on to say love is like this. It hides itself. It is not
to be gotten into words. The words change it—that is, the
literal words, the two-dimensional words on the page. And
yet she writes this poem *with* words, words that hopefully
go beyond the words.

This theme is of course one of the commonplaces of
poetry, though the "dimension" metaphor seems to be
novel. The third dimension, she says (and mostly it seems
like the fourth dimension), gets at us indirectly; we can
never quite spot it. It gets at us through art, through love,
through poetry, through Mr. Wheelwright's "Expressive."
And when it gets to us we have, lo, an epiphany.

I mention the Levertov poem because by analogy it
sets up a *relationship* between the Expressive and the
Literal. They are not opposed but complementary. You
won't find the third dimension without the other two. The
third dimension hides itself, as she says; it hides itself in
the other two. For example, you can't see the bulk of a
cube; you see its outside surfaces, and conjure up the bulk.

Our true zero poets—and unfortunately Miss Levertov
seems like one to me elsewhere—want the third dimension
alone. They preach a new that is not built on an old. They
want direct truths, instant epiphanies. It is my contention
that we can get to the Expressive only through the Literal.
Language is built upon the Literal, and poetry is Language.
We do not have the Expressive without the Literal, though
we may not have much with the Literal alone.

These are old observations, but they keep not being

heeded. Poetry must be at least as well written as prose. A poet is not a poet because he has flunked freshman composition. The heart must know the mind. Three comes after one and two. And so does the Self. And so do you.

D
dolls

"D" is for Dolls. Writers can be divided into those who manipulate experience like puppeteers, and those who suffer experience like puppets. The Gods and the Jobs. But the division is unreal. Any artistic act is manipulative in some measure, and also a suffering in some measure. A matter of degree.

A work of art *seems* manipulative—that is, seems like a puppet show—when it is badly manipulated, or when the artist deliberately *displays* his manipulative powers rather than trying to conceal them. I ask you to think of sophisticated puppetry in modern literature—of conscious manipulative displays, of instances where we find highly conventionalized images of humanity thrust at us with all their gears and wires showing: persons in masks and clown suits; grotesques, caricatures, baroquenesses. If you conduct a small survey, I think you will acknowledge that this "display" art has been as much a part of the modern scene as suffering reportage.

When I was in prep school my teachers gave me the word that literature had at last disposed of the decadent manipulators and was safely in the hands of realists. No more frivolous props, no more fooling around with dead forms, with masks, with puppets. Henceforward literature was destined to give us only the real and the true as 'twas lived. I digested this information and went on to college. There and thereafter I was introduced to various Gothic characters like Frankenstein and the creations of Poe, but I was also made aware that the puppetry genre went well beyond what was normally labeled "Gothic"—into Dickens, for example (Dickens was a great dollmaker), and later into Conrad, Ford, Faulkner and Golding, as well as into the work of many writers of science fiction. In the drama I was introduced to Alfred Jarry's *Ubu Roi,* but also to Walt Disney and Samuel Beckett. And in poetry I was introduced to, above all, Yeats.

Yeats sat in on the first performance of *Ubu Roi,* which is a sort of black *Babar,* in Paris in 1907; but long before that he had been close to many French and English manipulators, and was steeped in their platitudes about life imitating art. (Think of the one I mentioned earlier: "And as for living, our servants will do that for us.") He was familiar both with how they patched people together and how they mocked up a toylike nature for a backdrop. The tone of the following lines (from the play *Fantasio,* by Alfred de Musset, 1837) would have been commonplace to him:

What a failure this sunset is! Nature does wretchedly tonight. Look at that valley down there, those four or five measly clouds climbing the mountain. I used to do landscapes like that when I was twelve years old, on the cover of my schoolbooks.

But to these largely French conventions (what I will call not op art or pop art but "prop" art) Yeats brought many less sophisticated, less obviously molded or styled grotesques out of Irish mythology. And he brought along as well a disposition to be serious about his manipulations. In all, he had perhaps the oddest assortment of artistic and spiritual dolls in his attic of any modern poet.

I can't give a course in Yeats here, so I must simply assume your familiarity with his manipulations of history

and personality in *A Vision,* a book that adds up to a sort
of four-thousand-year puppet show, and then give you a
fragmentary anthology of puppetry in some of his poems.
First take the poem "The Dolls":

> A doll in the doll-maker's house
> Looks at the cradle and bawls:
> "That is an insult to us."
> But the oldest of all the dolls,
> Who had seen, being kept for show,
> Generations of his sort,
> Outscreams the whole shelf: "Although
> There's not a man can report
> Evil of this place,
> The man and the woman bring
> Hither, to our disgrace,
> A noisy and filthy thing."
> Hearing him groan and stretch
> The doll-maker's wife is aware
> Her husband has heard the wretch,
> And crouched by the arm of his chair,
> She murmurs into his ear,
> Head upon shoulder leant:
> "My dear, my dear, O dear,
> It was an accident."

Richard Ellmann notes that Yeats may have been thinking
of himself as the dollmaker here. I agree. The artist is
dollmaker, and he is very apt to take the side of his dolls,
and be annoyed and distracted by having something real
around the house, like a baby. On the other hand, as a
person he can also be annoyed at having to play dollmaker
all the time, be a dealer in dolls rather than experience.
Dolls are the artist's creations, the only humanity in his
artist's universe, and they get moved around on wires and
strings and keep being unsatisfactory, insufficient—an obsessive Yeatsian theme—because they are substitutes for,
rather than emanations of, real people. Remember his little

poem about what would have "shaken from the sieve" if he had married Maude Gonne and "been content to live." Think of his trips to Byzantium, think of his dozens of dream poems set uncomfortably against a rationalist modern Ireland, and think of all the recurrent play imagery in his work—god's death as a play, Chinese dancers unwinding history on a stage,* and so on. Finally, think of how his various props and constructs keep being qualified, denied:

> Many ingenious lovely things are gone
> That seemed sheer miracle to the multitude.
> *   *
> But all is changed, that high horse riderless,
> Though mounted in that saddle Homer rode,
> Where the swan drifts upon a darkening flood.
> *   *
> Now that my ladder's gone,
> I must lie down where all the ladders start,
> In the foul rag-and-bone shop of the heart.
> *   *
> A woman can be proud and stiff [like a puppet]
> When on love intent;
> But love has pitched his mansion
> In the place of excrement.

Then on the other side remember his frequent assertions of the *validity* of artifice. The end of "The Tower" is an instance; also "Lapis Lazuli." And recall how much of the force of Yeats' imagery depends upon its deliberate artificiality:

---

*I should note that Loie Fuller, the dancer referred to in "Nineteen Hundred and Nineteen," was a great prop artist in her own right. Far from being a "straight" dancer, she used all the stage effects she could think of. She even used sticks to hold her gowns out and make her assume various hopefully symbolic shapes. The bodies of her dancers were largely clothes hangers. Read Frank Kermode on this in *Puzzles and Epiphanies.*

THE MAGI*

Now as at all times I can see in the mind's eye
In their stiff, painted clothes, the pale unsatisfied ones
Appear and disappear in the blue depth of the sky
With all their ancient faces like rain-beaten stones,
And all their helms of silver hovering side by side,
And all their eyes still fixed, hoping to find once more,
Being by Calvary's turbulence unsatisfied,
The uncontrollable mystery on the bestial floor.

*   *

Put off that mask of burning gold
With emerald eyes.

*   *

I am worn out with dreams;
A weather-worn, marble triton
Among the streams.

*   *

He stretched his bones and fell in a dream
Of sun and moon that a good hour
Bellowed and pranced in the round tower;
Of golden king and silver lady
Bellowing up and bellowing round,
Till toes mastered a sweet measure,
Mouth mastered a sweet sound,
Prancing round and prancing up
Until they pranced upon the top.

*   *

When have I last looked on
The round green eyes and the long wavering bodies
Of the dark leopards of the moon?

*   *

---

*A characteristically casual Yeats footnote relates this poem to "The Dolls." He says that after he had written "The Dolls" (in which he was trying to observe how "all thought among us is frozen into something other than human life"), he looked up in the sky, saw "stiff figures in procession," and wrote a second "fable called 'The Magi,' complementary forms of those enraged dolls."

Bring where our Beauty lies
A new modelled doll, or drawing, . . .
We have given the world our passion,
We have naught for death but toys.

*   *

There all the golden codgers lay,
There the silver dew,
And the great water sighed for love,
And the wind sighed too.

So there: Yeats. I suppose the wonder of Yeats was that
he could sit in modern London or Dublin and talk about
golden codgers and leopards of the moon with a straight
face. The only other modern poet I know who has successfully done this sort of thing is Wallace Stevens, yet the
puppet art continues to rage around us. A student at Carleton recently wrote a very interesting pantomime, in which
all the actors wear masks and act like puppets. And a poet
named Russell Edson is writing many lines like these:

An old man got into a soup pot and shook a wooden
    spoon at the sky.
When he had finished he went upstairs to his room and
    died.
When his wife came home she said, stop being dead,
    there is no reason for it.

Then there's Lawrence Ferlinghetti:

In a surrealist year
            of sandwichmen and sunbathers
            dead sunflowers and live telephones
    housebroken politicos with party whips
    performed as usual
    in the rings of their sawdust circuses
    where tumblers and human cannonballs filled the
        air like cries . . .

Then of course there's Batman (though maybe not for
long). The examples could go on and on, in pop art,
and in the work of us "serious" poets too. I think I can see
some of the reasons. For example, our rebel poets dwell
constantly on the inhumanity of modern man, on his lack
of individuality, and so on. Hence in searching for ways
of describing him they gravitate toward puppets. The new
puppets are really reductions from the social sciences—the
commuter, the teen-ager, the FBI agent, the psychopath,
and so forth—and their essential outlines are so familiar to
us that the poet has to make his caricatures of them terribly extravagant or he will just be doing what Al Capp
does, or David Riesman. So he keeps insisting on the
thoroughly grotesque. But puppetry it remains, black puppetry. It's in.

I've already said that all art is manipulative. I might
add that Yeats, one of the great manipulators, is also my
favorite poet—for I don't want you to understand that I'm
against manipulation. Yet Yeats, who apparently was personally a great *poseur* (affinity with puppets), displayed an
awareness of the limits of poses, of manipulation—that is,
of the limits of art—that is absolutely essential to any great
art: an awareness of the suffering side, the Job side of art.
That awareness is as much a part of his work as the other.
He seesawed between the two. He brought us into the
dollhouse and said, Look.

Most of our new puppeteers fail to understand the
seesaw. Because they are blindly committed to show biz,
they keep looking like puppets themselves.

C
criticism and communion

I am told by Rilke, who always gets quoted on the subject, that there is no connection between the two:

Works of art are of an infinite loneliness and with nothing to be so little reached as with criticism.

So that is that. We have a vast critical machinery all tuned to the business of doing what it cannot do. The transaction first between poet and world, and second between poet and poet-lover (that is, audience), is not a critical transaction. Poor Brooks and Warren.

I doubt that Rilke's remark would be so popular if poetry hadn't been getting such a workout in our classrooms. Many of our classroom operations should be performed instead on works not worth our love, for the operations *are* dangerous to poetry. We need another classroom revolution, and soon, for many, though not all, of the good things that a good critic can say about language could be said about our muscular and corrupt public rhetoric instead, leaving poetry alone. What began as a pedagogical procedure has gotten out of hand and come to affect the poetry more than the students. Collectively our critics and teachers have alienated our poets—and that is sufficient evidence for me that the system is at least partly wrong.

But, if I may argue with Rilke, the faults in our system should not be construed to mean that criticism cannot "reach" poetry. It can; it frequently does. I take it as a first principle of criticism that poetry, good poetry, is accessible to a good mind; and as a corollary to that principle, that the mind and the heart are not two different countries. If these propositions are acknowledged, it is difficult to avoid the conclusion that a good critic, playing the role of teacher, can *help* to make poetry accessible to other minds, or train other minds in the ways of accessibility, just as he can train them in any other mental operations. That we now overteach like mad should not be used as evidence that we cannot teach at all.

Put it differently: Rilke is right and wrong. He is wrong in saying that criticism cannot reach poetry, for the critic can be a lover too, and his criticism an act of love. But he is right in denying the critic the power to pass love on to another. I cannot tell a student to love a poem; I can only describe, so that he will understand, the road by which I came there. Love is the part of the transaction between poet and reader that the critic-intermediary cannot control. When he tries to control it we have a case of overteach. Brooks-and-Warren criticism is sometimes a case of overteach. The procedures enunciated by it are impressive, but the attitude of the true advocates of it is ultimately prescriptive; that is, it is prescriptive about matters that the student has to write the prescriptions for.

I am not, you see, really talking about criticism and its relation to poetry, but about our educational system. There's so much of it; no end to it. We are being *taught*, cradle to grave. What are we learning? And why does poetry bear so much of the burden of the *teaching* of the language when the poetry is above all that which has to be learned?

These are fuzzy distinctions. It is impossible to specify in any complicated educational situation how much of what is taught is learned (or how much of what is not taught is learned!); yet the distinction between teaching and learning is of greater importance in poetry than elsewhere, for Rilke's reason.

I would think that the best criticism in our age of

overteach would be suggestive, incomplete, fragmentary, for Rilke's reason. The good critic of poetry should lead the educators away from packaged education where packaged education is not working. The New Criticism is not working, so the critic's job now would seem to be to oppose it.

But in defense of the New Criticism I must acknowledge that its theoretical strength is that it is *not* prescriptive but inductive; it is intended only to lead to the curtained door behind which the girl lies, not put the student in bed with her. It *discourages* the student from accepting other people's accounts of the girl as equivalent to an affair with her. And though the New Criticism is in trouble, it remains the strongest defense we have against the extreme prescriptiveness of some of its opponents. Out in the badlands of anti-academia the alternatives to the New Criticism pad about like wild apes. Each arrogant, aggressive, envious, self-centered, self-styled poet would have his own school, his own magazine, his own prescriptions and his own arsenal of epithets to demolish other ape schools, ape mags, ape poets. The more difficult it becomes to judge a poem, the more shrill and positive and numerous are the judgments. Under these conditions the cool rationality of the New Criticism remains something not to be sneezed at even if it is not saving the world.

But what can we do with the New Criticism to make it more effective, or less prescriptive, less addicted to the vice it was designed to combat? My solution at the moment is an old one, one I would simply like to see revived. I see possibilities for indulging in the kind of investigation into the *origins* of the poetic act that the New Criticism has mostly opposed. Aestheticians describe my interest as the genetic fallacy—going back into the poet's life to examine the conditions under which the poems were written. It is a fallacy, I am told, because the preliminary conditions for the writing of a poem have no bearing upon the value of the finished poem. To deal with poetry as a manifestation of behavior is to deny poetry as an art.

Very well. Suppose we were to deny poetry as an art for a bit. Or not deny it, simply play down the art, interest ourselves in its humanity. Would that be so bad? Then we might practice what I will call "underground" criticism, perhaps practice it extensively with bad poems, but practice it to see what makes them and their authors tick.

Some poets and critics take great offense at such procedures—that's the trouble. They think of what a sociologist does with "The Waste Land," or a Freudian with the Romantics. They note that these things have been done many times, and done badly. They remember mostly the bad times, for those are the ones they want to remember; they would preserve criticism for the exploration of values rather than of social or psychological conditions. Among other things, the New Criticism was in its infancy a sharp reaction against the encroachments of the social sciences upon art, and the hard feelings are still around (recently at a meeting Allen Tate mentioned the social sciences, and then added, "if there is such a thing").

Let me suggest that between the behaviorists and the value people there's a sort of no-man's land to which little attention is paid, where on the one hand the artistic values of poets are of considerable behavioral interest (how did the poets get to entertain such values?), and on the other their behavior is of considerable artistic import (what are our values based on?). Take genres, forms, conventions, all those preliminary artistic conditions that are also behavioral conditions. The New Critics pass over them as fast as they can (after granting the need for a little preliminary background) to get to the "work itself," while the behaviorists spend all their time with them and never get to the "work itself." Between is where the interdisciplinary act needs to be practiced, yet I can't think of many prominent literary critics who are now working to illuminate what goes on in the poet's Kasserine Pass aesthetically, morally, psychologically, and socially as he settles to his job of getting his poem "right." That area has been abandoned, and abandoned in a period of greater uncertainty about the function and worth of art than any I can name.

What do Brooks and Warren do in the Kasserine Pass? They pick the problem up when the poet has already established his intentions in the poem, and is working on various drafts of it (see what they do with a Housman poem, "The Immortal Part," for example, in the back of *Understanding Poetry*). They come into close focus, then, on the various artistic or craftsman decisions the poet makes as he moves from draft to draft. This is fine, and if it would only encourage young poets to go through more drafts than they do it would be very helpful. It is fine as far as it goes, but it keeps genetics in the realm of art. If we are going to be genetical, we should at least indulge the genetic fallacy thoroughly. I want to talk with the poet as well as with his poetry.

They would hate me for this. How severe the New Critics' strictures are about critical relevance is well indicated by Allen Tate's account of the writing of his own poem, "Ode to the Confederate Dead." In his essay about it, called "Narcissus as Narcissus," Tate was in the best of all possible positions to talk about the presumably narcissistic genetics of the poem; but despite the title, he didn't. He rejected the possibility at the outset of his essay, and in fact delivered himself of a small complaint against genetic criticism before going on to discuss the poem in perfectly sound and impersonal Brooks-and-Warren fashion. The essay is informative. I find it also inhuman, that is, not giving of Tate's own humanity, a humanity most pleasingly conspicuous in many of his theoretically less personal essays.

I keep plugging for the humanity of poetry. This is tiresome, and you may think unnecessary. Looking at what's happening in poetry, I don't find it unnecessary. The burden of my account here has been that most of the current modes of poetry and criticism give us a poetry that is separatist, give us a poetry that is a game, poetry that is puppetry, poetry that is technical novelty. I have respect for these views; I think a gamesman's approach to art is a necessary preliminary to the understanding of art, like mastering the Literal before mushing off into the Expressive. But I'm also desperately tired of game theory that keeps trying to take over poetry completely. It seems to me that this is what Rilke's complaint was all about.

B

"B" is an interlude before "A." "B" is for Beloit. I like Beloit. I'm very grateful to Beloit. I thank Beloit for inviting me. I'm very sorry for Beloit for what it has had to put up with from me in the last week.

A
absolute

Now "A." Here we are at the end of the backward alphabet, with nothing to worry about but the Absolute. It must be clear that I'm not an absolutist—or if one, a poor soft-headed example of one. I feel about absolutes the way I feel about zero: one way of staying alive is keeping away from the ends of the alphabet.

I pretty well emptied out my thoughts on the absolute while talking about music. But here goes. I regard the absolutes we think we have in the arts—things like the *Mona Lisa*—as kept absolutes. I'm not against keeping things. If I were I wouldn't have settled in the humanities, disciplines largely based on keeping things. But I'm against keeping things the way squirrels do, automatically. We have extraordinary facilities that squirrels don't have for keeping things; we can see to it that the world's worst sonnet never rots in the ground. We spend so much time and energy in acts of preserving that we can't make room for the problem of what we should preserve, much less for reading and enjoying what we preserve. The result is that much of what passes for art of enduring value is enduring because it has been kept in a glass case. I know how hard it is to decide what should be kept and what should not be kept, but I don't see that this difficulty makes it reasonable for us to turn the responsibility for deciding over to glass cases. The glass-case theory of art—which is certainly prevalent in our English departments, and in our graduate schools in English—is a prescriptive theory. In effect we say to ourselves that we ought to have absolutes; therefore we will have them. By the billions. In museums.

Do I exaggerate with billions? Maybe, in glass cases.

But think of microfilm. We do have microfilm. Just the other day I got in the mail a brochure promoting the sale of 25,000 American and British plays of the nineteenth century on microfilm. 25,000! They were to come at me at the rate of four hundred a month for several years. What an opportunity!

If I were given a free hand in our museums, libraries, and courses I wouldn't range around with fire and ax like Attila the Hun, but I would try to make sure that at least as much energy and intelligence were devoted to reducing our holdings in art as to holding and disseminating them, my principle being (aside from a wistful, hopeless yearning for traveling light) that values in art are no less evolutionary than we are. We need to know a bit about pterodactyls, but we do not need to keep telling ourselves that they are still alive and kicking. As for poetry, I much regret that in an age when we have for the first time learned a great deal about social and psychological evolution, most literary critics seem to be back in Tennessee with William Jennings Bryan. I see a great intellectual fallacy here at work about the nature of art, and I also, as I have said, see a great deal of inhumanity at work. Out of the world of the nightmare, which is perfectly human; out of the improbable ideals of children and commonfolk, who are perfectly human; and out of the confusing collectivist world of supermarket and nation, which is also, I must insist, perfectly human—inexplicably out of all this for several decades we have been constructing theories of poetry that are essentially inhuman, that are loaded with denials of humanity, that are rigged. The poetic revolution is backfiring. Our art is getting artier and artier even as it professes to be leading the human parade. And behind all this artistic inhumanity I see the dark art-god of the absolute, still egging us on, telling us to keep on with the search for values beyond momentary values, telling us to find It.

I reject this art-god, but I doubt that I would be posing as a poet at all if I didn't share with those who heed him a sense that evolution, or the idea of evolution, has gotten out of hand. It is obvious that we tend to confuse evolution with fashion, to confuse that big, slow, mysterious thing with the latest trends in women's clothes. Much existentialism seems to come to this, and I have as little time for it as I do for the dark god. Though the world moves, it moves at more than one speed, and we should no more confuse the speed of art with the day-by-day cultural pace as we read of it in the newspapers, or as we live it existentially in our cellars, than we should imagine that art has no speed at all.

Put it differently: I do have sympathies with the critics' respectable efforts to hang on to poetry as a place of relative permanence, or a way to relative permanence, in the flux; but my sympathies are flagging. I'm becoming an infidel because I've seen so much nonsense put forth on the subject.

I remember a long time ago being one of the faithful, and being much annoyed by a professor of philosophy at Yale, F. S. C. Northrop, for describing poets—and he threw in English teachers—as unreliable purveyors of values. His line was that the poet is not a disciplined thinker, not an aesthetician, not a philosopher, not a notable representative of rationality (like Northrop). Plato, of course, felt the same way, and I was mad at him too—but this whole argument now seems to me to be a tempest in a teapot. I was offended that Northrop could set himself up, by implication, as the purveyor of ultimate values; now it seems to me obvious that neither philosopher nor poet can do so. No one can do so.

Oddly, it seems to me that the poet did not attempt to do so until recent times. Ours is the great age of the artist flying solo—or thinking he can. A while back most poets would have acknowledged the priority, as it were, of other minds than their own, or at least the priority of other parts of their own minds than the poetic part. Call this classicism. By its principles the working artist regards himself as what Northrop would still have him, a "handmaiden" to established forces outside himself. It was only when the philosophers and priests faltered in their authoritarianism that the role of contemporary artists in the *determination* of value began to be aggressively asserted.

We have no handmaiden artists now. The arrogance of our poets seems to be the one stable factor in what Northrop Frye has described as a sort of literary stock exchange, with the reputations of poets regularly booming and crashing all around. How we keep arriving at such pontifical certainties in the midst of so much uncertainty is amazing to me, and I would be inclined to whisper to you that really poets have become very corrupt, have become just smart brokers in art fashions, if I were not worried about that word "corrupt." For to talk of corruption—as any artist does when he sees some new artistic hot-air balloon sailing heavenward in the newspapers—is to imply the possibility of a state of purity, a place of value and incorruptibility residing outside the range of the cultural flux. All through these lectures I've been trying to avoid acknowledging such a possibility, partly because I don't believe in it and partly because I think the quest for the removed value has dulled our sense of the human condition. It is in the quest for purity that we begin to indulge our fallacy of artistic autonomy, begin to imagine platonist nooks, begin to blind ourselves to what we have and what we are. So I will not have it that poets are corrupt, only blinded by the problems of their specialty, and confused by the world's high hopes for their specialty.

I can't see any way out of the confusion except by the continuing cultivation of a respect for the Other. The here-and-now Other.

Not some Absolute Other, some Zero Other. The

trouble with the Absolute is that we can't *see* its shape, its dimensions, its character. We have to conjure it up, give it its character; and that tends to trap us with ourselves. The here-and-now Other is the one we find with our senses every day, the one we live with and feel the real Otherness of. I'm very Western on this point (having met so many newly converted Eastern psyches in my short stay on the Beloit campus). It seems to me that a respect for the Other is an imperative across the board. It's an intellectual imperative: no scientist can tell the crayfish what it is, the crayfish tells him. It's a social imperative, built into a sound aristocracy, a sound democracy, any healthy communal situation. It's certainly a marital imperative, a love imperative. And it's an artistic imperative. We can't violate the tree we describe; it isn't ours to violate. We can't violate the language we use; it isn't ours to violate. We have to come to terms with that tree or that language, and we have also to come to terms with the audience for the tree we have put into language. We can't just order these forces around, but must in some sense always serve them, serve them honestly without regard for the self-consequences. I can't see that any poetic transaction with the Other will come to much without this respect, without this notion of service.

PART II

PART II

5

THE LIMITATIONS OF
REASON:

Or, How Can We Get from One to Two?

A LONG TIME AGO John Milton showed us what was wrong
with making the worse out as the better cause; you know,
he showed us that Satan wasn't as good as God, though
Satan wanted heaven to think he was. Those of you who
are really learned about Milton probably know too the odd
literary argument which makes Satan the "real" hero of
Paradise Lost. This argument sympathizes with Satan because he got stuck with being judged on God's terms; that
is, it notes that Milton always left Satan standing for the
bad words in God's vocabulary—standing for the worst or
lowest or least when, if Satan had had his way, the very
word "Satan" would have come to stand for something
nifty. Some people would say it was all a semantic rather
than a moral problem—they're Satanists perhaps.

My mission here is somehow to celebrate academic
excellence. It would therefore be unmannerly of me to be
a Satanist and try to make the grade of "E," rather than
"A," an honor. I won't. I do want to complain, however,
about the instability of our grading systems, in the hope
that I will persuade you to worry about the standards by
which the world's "A's" are awarded.

We have many, many grading systems, some of which
we don't even think of as grading systems. A chess player

can get to be a grand master, a football player can get to be all-American, a murderer can get on the list of the FBI's Ten Most Wanted criminals. All these are "A's" in their way, as are the various awards given for baking cakes, raising pigs, and performing acts of heroism in war; and all of them are awarded as a result of applying certain standards of measurement appropriate for the occasion. We do not measure chess masters for their cakes; we do not measure cake bakers for their chess. If we are to measure our chess players and cake bakers accurately, we must first agree on what we are measuring—that is, define what "A" is and what "E" is in chess and cakes—and then stick to the definition for the duration of the measuring process.

But the more important the qualities we are trying to measure, the more difficult is the process of defining these qualities. On the academic scene, for example, what sort of student would we most like to have at Lawrence or Carleton? Good students, of course, but good at what? In what way good? Shall we define the good in terms of cake baking? Chess? Football? Performance on College Board exams? Character? This is, I suppose, an admissions problem, and I bring it up because recently at Carleton we have had a big discussion of what a good prospective student is, and have found ourselves battling, not over the word "good" (that's been done), but over the word "positive." Somehow or other there crept into a newspaper article describing Carleton's admissions procedures the word "positive"; Carleton, it said, was looking for students who were "positive." From the article it looked as if we were setting out to give "A's" for effort, to make "good" and "positive" synonymous. Furthermore, right next to the word "positive" in this article appeared an ambiguous description of some students somebody had thought to be negative, negative because they had been criticizing Carleton's administration in the undergraduate newspaper. We had quite a ruckus about that: a lot of Carleton students, and some faculty members too, began to be like Satan; they began to *pride* themselves on being negative.

The only reason for anybody to want to be bad rather than good, or to want an "E" rather than an "A," or to want to be negative rather than positive, is that he objects to the grading system by which he is being measured. But as you all know, we have thousands of cases of such questioning of our standards of measurement cropping up around us all the time. Ours is a world where it is hard to find any standards of consequence that have not been or are not being called into question constantly. Furthermore these questionings, as in the recent case at Carleton, are usually not only questionings about the standards of measurement but about those who establish those standards, that is, the authorities, whoever they may be. A cynic could propose that the signification of all value words is entirely determined by the whims of the powers-that-be in any given culture, so that ultimately we are all faced with the kind of thing that George Orwell describes in 1984, where the administration may, if it so chooses, determine that black is white, white black. An idealist would of course deny this, and find a source of authority outside the dean's office, perhaps in heaven. A humanist might also deny the whimsical character of our measurement systems by referring to the standards which his *culture* has developed over the centuries, standards not to be overturned or revised by any individual administration. But both the idealist and the humanist would, I think, be obliged to admit that there has probably never been a time when the cultural or moral values we have inherited have been disturbed so regularly and with such vehemence and from so many quarters as they are now being disturbed. Authority in all its forms is constantly being called into question; so it is little wonder that the authority of value words like "A" or "good" or "positive" should be, similarly, suspect.

The value word I am most interested in here is a word

you might not think of at first as a value word. Reason. The word has a good many meanings, some of which are not necessarily value meanings. Thus it is possible to talk about reason as opposed to feeling without necessarily giving reason an "A" and feeling an "E." And we can also talk about the reasoning *process* (induction, deduction, all that) without alleging that it is either a good or a bad process. Yet in fact the word is seldom used without some connotations of value; it tends to be a purr word (that is, a word of praise) among scientists and administrators, and a curse word among poets and lovers. The argument here is an old one, going back to Plato; but if we put it in its modern context, and think of reason and reasonableness in the large, with all their connotations like common sense and sobriety, we see that they are value words for more than scientists and administrators. All the middle-class virtues having to do with being moderate and responsible and normal tend to congregate around reasonableness.

No wonder then that our rebels—poets, lovers, pacifists, "E" students, political revolutionaries, beats, you name them—no wonder that they tend to take the word "reason" as a curse word. Reason stands for the powers that be; reason is administrative reason, a late form of what Milton called right reason. So our rebels, like Satan, searching about for an opposite, have found themselves standing for the abnormal, the irresponsible, the negative, the sick, the *ir*rational.

Most literary people are annoyed when upright citizens go about calling modern literature irrational, irresponsible, negative or sick, but they don't mind much when the characterizations come from literary people themselves (one instance is Karl Shapiro's book *In Defense of Ignorance*). One can imagine a similar confusion in hell, with the citizens there amicably describing each other as devils until an angel comes along with the same description. Then outrage. The angel's righteous Miltonic tone will cause part of the trouble, but another part will be the result of the word "devil" itself, which presumably has different meanings for angels and devils. For angels, devils are bad people, but for devils, devils are *my* people.

Is it possible to divorce the social, political, cultural connotations of a big value word like "reason" from the denotative meaning of such a word? Probably not. The meaning of words *is* a social and cultural matter—that is, a matter inseparable from usage—and if the dean establishes what is reasonable, there are always going to be students who want to be unreasonable because they don't like the dean's usage. Yet there are, it seems to me, some long-term meanings for the word "reason" that it is fairly stupid for even the wildest rebel to object to; in a way, the rebel is throwing away his whole cause by letting the administration have the word. Better that he fight for it. Sometimes I think rebels would benefit by a few vocabulary exercises, not in the hope that they can change the course of language but in the hope that they can keep the language from coming all over them.

Maybe my statements here are coming to seem like a confusing vocabulary exercise. Let me take a different tack. Looking at the word "reason" loosely, I think it is fair to say that there are two basically opposed views of the word's meaning. One is the limited view that prescribes that reason be thought of as logic or some other restricted, gamey, according-to-the-rules notion of mental activity. If, for example, one looks up "reason" in the 11th edition of the *Encyclopaedia Britannica*, one notes that only one column is devoted to reason, at the end of which one is referred to logic, which takes up forty dense pages. Or if one thinks of reason simply as reasonableness or common sense, then similarly a restriction (a social or cultural restriction) is placed upon the notion of rational activity: rational activity is then that which society or culture regards as sensible or perhaps inoffensive. But the other view of reason is that it is simply thought itself, thought being everything that goes on in the mind of man. Thus when Hamlet says to Horatio that there are more things in heaven and earth than are covered by his philosophy, Hamlet is taking this latter, broader view and saying of Horatio that he doesn't understand the possible dimensions of human thought.

Imagine pages and pages here on this point, at the end of which we have these two clear and opposed views of the word "reason," one restrictive and one expansive. A restrictive reasoner would give Hamlet an "E" as a rational being; an expansive reasoner would give him an "A." In parenthesis, I should say that I think this absolute distinction is incorrect. I don't see that reason can ever be interpreted to be simply random thought. The notion of limits, of restriction, of the imposition of some sort of order or form upon thoughts, seems to me to be a part of both the restrictive and expansive view of the word; so I am really talking about a difference of degree rather than of kind. I'll return to this.

Shakespeare wrote more eloquently on this subject than anybody, but another man who came close was Jonathan Swift, an expansive rationalist whose fourth Gulliver book, *A Voyage to the Land of the Houyhnhnms*, fits my occasion well. Swift, like Hamlet, had trouble coping with restrictive rationalists, and the Houyhnhnm book seems to be quite specifically a discussion of the dimensions of reason.

The Houyhnhnms themselves—that is, the horses—are the restrictive rationalists of the piece. Their limitations or restrictions are too frequently ignored by readers in favor of their virtues, but the limitations are unquestionably there. The limitations of these wise horses are both experiential and moral. The limitations of their experience prevent them from inferring the possibility of a land outside their own, or from conceding the possible physical virtues of species other than their own. They don't even have any *interest* in possibilities outside their own frame of reference; they have no interest in human nature or society; they have no words for "Power, Government, War, Law, Punishment and a thousand other things." As for their moral deficiencies, these too are indicated by their deficient vocabulary: they have no words to express lying or falsehood or even doubt. They sit around in continuous astonishment and indignation as Gulliver describes human vice, and toward the end they seriously consider a proposal for eliminating vice and irrationality in the world by simply exterminating the Yahoos.

Gulliver, on the other hand, is reasonable in the expansive sense, though unlike Hamlet he doesn't realize it. That is, he is worldly-wise, knowledgeable, loaded down with information about human beings (all of which is bad). He runs rings around the Houyhnhnms, without realizing it, in simple awareness of how things are in the world. So he could well be our rational hero here if it were not for his one fatal flaw; he has been sold a bill of goods by somebody—say the restrictive rationalists of his own society—so that he takes as his ideal the restrictive rationalism of the Houyhnhnms and is accordingly depressed by the inability of human beings to live within those restrictions. To put it crudely, he, though a man whose whole experience, like any human being's, has told him that syllogisms will not order the world, nonetheless proposes to himself that they should, and so goes on to identify himself with the Houyhnhnms. He does so so completely that he comes to wish to have nothing more to do with humanity at all; he would rather live within a syllogism.

Now where is Swift in all this? Swift I take to be an expansive rationalist with no illusions about the sufficiency of syllogisms for explaining and ordering human life. Swift, I would say, is telling us that there is nothing more irrational than a rationale that leads a human being to deny his own humanity; he reinforces this point by having the

humane captain who rescues Gulliver conclude that Gulliver's misfortunes had impaired his reason. What, specifically, is the rational impairment?—Adopting, I would say,
the Houyhnhnms' limited *meaning* for reason.

Now, my subject is not Swift here, but the dimensions
of reason in our time, and I would not belabor Swift's
book if I did not think it relevant. It is. We can find the
same cast of characters—or various versions of this cast—
in our world; there is nothing archaic about them. Think
of all the rationalists in different fields who adhere to the
intensive rationalist view, that is, to the horses' view, the
limited view of the nature of reason. All specialists in all
fields may be said to be of this character whenever they
come to let their own particular specialties control their
view of the whole of life.

As for Gulliver, well, most of us have a bit of Gulliver in us, and we display it whenever we are faced with
successful rational specialists. We fawn before the successes of concentration, the masters of any kind of syllogism, the champions at chess or theoretical physics. And
our judgment of their success is based on the limited mea-
surements for success within the special fields. I, for example, as a poet and literary editor, make decisions about
the works of my contemporaries—that is, give them "A's"
and "E's"—only by dealing with a fairly narrow range of
poetic factors. I assume that similarly the mathematician
or the biologist or the philosopher is limited in his capacity
to adjudicate, as it were, between the requirements of a
limited vision and those of an expansive vision. To put it
another way, we not only do not seem to have many Swifts
and Shakespeares in our time (the possibilities for attain-
ing their comprehension seem now very remote), but we
also have little capacity for recognizing them when and if
they appear. We have to give our "A's" and "E's" in places
where we have means for evaluation, and increasingly those

means are not available to us outside what we call the "field
of our concentration."

Occasionally we find spectacular crossovers. C. P. Snow
gave F. R. Leavis an "E," and Leavis returned the compli-
ment. But for the most part our battles about standards
take place *within* individual disciplines or professions: politician against politician, poet against poet, scientist against
scientist. And the Gullivers of the world, similarly restricted,
find their Houyhnhnms and their Yahoos *within* the discipline of their choice.

Need I say that such a condition raises hell with the
notion of a liberal arts college? In college we call the disciplines or specialties departments, but the name doesn't
matter; the condition remains. We may talk a lot about
breadth of education, but the talk is mostly outside
the curriculum. Inside the curriculum the fences are up;
and as the student progresses toward graduate work the
fences get higher and higher. The general education
courses, the interdisciplinary courses, the great-books
courses—these are the things to get over. When you really
get going, you begin to *concentrate*—and that means to
accept wholeheartedly the limited rational vision.

As a sort of amateur educator, without a Ph.D., and
without any great capacity for concentration anyway, I
have been worrying for a long time about such problems,
and I have made a number of discoveries. I have discovered,
for example, that my own discipline, literature, though
theoretically one of the expansive disciplines, is actually
one of the most restrictive. I bleed for it, and find that,
partly because of its modern restrictions, I tend as I grow
older to move out from literature—that is, out from the
regular canon that we teach all the time, from Chaucer to
T. S. Eliot—into a number of fields that are looked upon
as enemy territory by many literary people—you know, sociology, international relations, and so on. I have also gotten

interested in the problems of making our curricular offerings more interdisciplinary—and this interest has also led some of my colleagues to look at me with some astonishment and remorse. Let me report my findings.

In the first place the arguments *for* the concentrations we have, that is, for the fifteen or twenty restricted departments that make up the average small college—the arguments for these concentrations, though I don't like them, are very strong. Within them we do have standards for measurement; the standards in English are less precise than in Math—nobody has ever really learned quite how to grade a freshman theme—but the standards are nonetheless there, and we have been developing them, refining them for generations. As a result, within our respective closets we know what we are doing, more or less, and to those who complain about the dimensions of our closets we say that it is better to live rationally in the closets than irrationally outside them.

Nor are we wholly unaware of what goes on outside the closets. We peer out quite a bit, and what we see is very depressing. Let me give you a sample of the sort of thing we see outside, a statement from a person with a very expansive rational vision:

Man is in the process of developing a new consciousness, which, in spite of his apparent spiritual and moral captivity, can eventually lift the human race above and beyond the fear, ignorance and isolation which beset it today. . . . Beyond the divisiveness among men there exists a primordial unitive power since we are all bound together by a common humanity more fundamental than any unity of dogma. . . . Mankind can finally place its trust not in a proletarian authoritarianism, not in a secularized humanism . . . but in a sacramental brotherhood and in the unity of knowledge.

Now I simply don't know what statements like that mean. It is not, but it sounds very much like one of those statements from the promoters of LSD. Statements like that drive me back into my closet in two shakes; they are simply too expansive for me. I am not trying to make fun of the statement when I say this, for I certainly wish that I could believe in some primordial unitive power, in the unity of knowledge, in a sacramental brotherhood. I would also like to imagine a *curriculum* that would lead students toward such unity, as well as a life outside the academies that would be intellectually less divisive, partitional. But I don't think we are going to achieve such unity, or even make modest steps toward it, merely by taking LSD or some equally synthetic equivalent and then putting forth big propositions about our capacity to do so. Such propositions keep reminding me of the little engine that could. Here we are back at "A" for effort again. In the childish world of the little engine that could, the "A's" and "E's" are measured in terms of the student's disposition or temperament. Is he positive or negative? Does he have a healthy or unhealthy attitude?—and I confess that I would rather be surrounded by classes and classes of diseased and closeted but bright skeptics than healthy, positive, wide-open-spaces idiots. If the expansive rational vision involves leaving out the vision, leaving out the rationality, leaving out one's perception of the terribly complex and unmalleable nature of things—then it is not an expansive vision at all, but an expansive blindness.

On the other hand, most teachers who advocate keeping what we have—that is, keeping the specialist system going—as well as people outside the academies who believe that our society is ultimately best off by being a society of many discrete parts bound loosely together by rubber bands and Scotch tape—people who believe in this mostly *do* make sense. They are rational; they are hardheaded; they don't take any wooden nickels; they do have standards for doling out the "A's" and "E's." They know very well that it is the privilege of only a pitiful few to be able to see things steadily and see them whole. And so their retreat into their closets is in a way a perfectly respectable act of intellectual humility, beside which the actions of some of our expansionists frequently seem arrogant and foolhardy. To recognize the limitations of man's rational capacity is at least as important as trying to expand them; thus part of Gulliver's error was in expecting too much. Remember how disillusioned he was at the end of the Houyhnhnms book when he discovered, six months after his return to England, that none of the reforms he had proposed for England had taken root. Such disillusionment would never have set in if he had been a rational skeptic in the first place.

Aside from the basic soundness of being hardheaded and recognizing limitations, there is another good reason for holding on to what we have, namely, that we haven't, in our democratic society, any very rational devices or machinery for extensive rational reform. On a campus, for example, when we undertake to revise the curriculum, our only recourse is to a committee. You all know the jokes about committees: What is a camel? A camel is an animal that looks as if it had been made by a committee; and so on. Committees are a necessary democratic phenomenon; we cannot do without them. But it is one thing to point to the political necessity of committees, and another to set committees the job of doing a society's most difficult thinking for it. The expansive rational vision that each intelligent, mature individual should, I suspect, at least take as an ideal to be worked toward is not to be achieved by putting five or twenty minds into the same lounge and telling them to go to work. What they come out with is not a fusion or rational synthesis of their respective visions and talents—not unity of knowledge, not sacramental brotherhood—but a compromise, an averaging out of these visions until all definition, all sharpness, is lost. Just as the statistician may make the ridiculous discovery that the average

American family has two and a half children, a faculty committee arguing about some simple problem—say whether
or not to have Saturday classes—will after great turmoil
recommend that classes be held every other Saturday. The
difficulties of committees are evident not only in the wishy-
washiness of the proposals they come up with but also by
the language they end up proposing the proposals with.
There's a fine parody of committee language going around,
in which the Gettysburg Address is redone as a committee
would have done it; it goes in part like this (there's also a
version of the same address as Eisenhower would have
done it): "Between 86 and 88 years prior to the formation
of this committee, our interdisciplinary predecessors in-
stigated in this area a new national concept centered around
a socio-economico-politico formula for liberationizing and
equalization of individual participants in our cultural syn-
drome."

Are there sensible ways of rational expansion? A good
many of our rebels say No. They say that the standards
we have are false, that we are living in a dream, or a hundred million dreams, of reason, and the only real solution
is to get those dreams out of our heads. Karl Shapiro, whom
I've already referred to as an example of a literary rebel,
has a rather nice poem to this effect which begins, "Lower
the standards; that's my motto." A good many persons
share this notion in one way or another; they think that
we must positively cultivate unreason if we are ever to get
rid of all the false, closet reasons we have. And so they do.
Not only do they rebel against whatever rational authorities
or rational orders they are surrounded by—this is their
negative side—but in being positive they insist upon being,
if they are poets or painters, surrealistic—that is, deliberately
avoiding *sense*, which is actually very hard to do—or, if
they are not artistically inclined, in simply living the good
life of an animal, which also is very hard to do.

I sympathize with a good bit of this, even though I

have a strong rationalistic background and bent, and I think we may have to do a modest amount of violence to some of our more ridiculous rational structures if we are to avoid having them do great violence to us. For example, I think that graduate training in the humanities is not for the most part humanistic any more, if it ever was, and that *there* is a dream of reason that needs to be, somehow, scotched. Yet as a rational being, or a professer to reason, I can't go very far with my idle schemes of violence because I do not believe, as my rebel friends do, that there is much profit to be derived from tearing down a rational structure, no matter how ridiculous, if you have no rational alternative for it. Unreason, as I see it, is simply not an alternative for a human being, though it may be all right for beasts of the field. Hence I haven't much time either for surrealistic poets or for other kinds of mental anarchists—revision not destruction is my motto.

From my own rational closet, to get down for a moment to cases, I can contemplate only very limited revisions. As a teacher of rhetoric, for example, I can imagine knocking down one wall of my closet into, say, history, and literally combining some history teacher's closet with mine in the teaching of how to write. To do this I would have to take some history, the history teacher would have to take some rhetoric; we would both be involved in what is known as teacher education, with the noble aim of combining in small measure our own rational structures and then passing on the results to our students. It is notorious, you know, how badly Americans write, and this is not because, or not entirely because, English teachers are not earning their keep, but because students don't think they have to write English when they are not *in* English. No successful reform for the teaching of writing in this country will come out of English departments, that is, English departments alone. What is needed is a kind of teacher-by-teacher infiltration of other-than-English departments *by* English departments, a limited, and hopefully controlled, expansion of the domain of that rational structure we sometimes call the art of rhetoric. At the same time, hopefully, the domain of English departments would be, step by step, invaded. I won't elaborate here upon what English departments should be invaded *with*—sometimes I think they should be invaded by all the waters of the seven seas—but simply emphasize again the notion of limited expansion or invasion, and go on to one other example from my own rational closet.

I'm the editor of a little magazine, a literary magazine; there are hundreds of these in our country. Mostly their circulations are under a thousand; they print stories and poems that are read, if they are read at all, by poets and short-story writers. The editors of these magazines, like myself, are constantly lamenting the limited range of their audience; they would like to be expansive; they blame the scientists or the sociologists or their neighborhood druggist —*any*body—for having given us a culture no longer interested in literature, new literature. Recently they even started an association of literary magazines—I was one of the founders—dedicated to the proposition that what these magazines needed was better distribution and promotion.

The association was a good idea. I was for it; I still am. But what the association and its members have so far neglected is that one of the main causes for the diminutive size of their closet is their own vision, not their public's. With them I would like to do what I would like to do with our rhetoric classes. I'd like to knock out a wall between the editor of a little literary magazine and the editor of, say, a bird magazine or a magazine about the sex habits of the Tahitians. Wouldn't it be great, I keep thinking idly, if I could arrange to combine an issue of the *Carleton Miscellany* with an issue of the *Bulletin of Atomic Scientists*?

Maybe it wouldn't be great; I don't know; and I don't plan to burden you here with any other specific schemes that I have for expanding my own particular rational vision, or that of my fellow editors and teachers of composition. My subject is not my own field, or closet, but, really, the essence of closets and how to change it.

To put it simply, the human mind is the basic closet. Four billion committees, ten thousand grants from Carnegie and Ford for interdisciplinary experiments and schemes for combating specialization, will accomplish nothing if, first, the individual isn't willing to experiment with getting out of his own closet.

The unpleasant fact is that not many individuals are willing to experiment, not at least after they have achieved maturity. The whole maturing process is away from the experimental, inventive actions and thoughts of the child to the surenesses, the standards of some given grown-up closet.

Worse, those few who are willing to experiment—and these are the ones I am interested in—are frequently not the best individuals to conduct experiments—and by "best" here I mean those most capable of developing an expansive rationalism. They get out of their closet mostly because they are incapable of doing very well inside it, and so they go off to do not very well elsewhere either.

Even worse, those few who are both willing to experiment and intellectually equipped to do so are not, in our society, given much encouragement for doing so. The only real, everyday, working alternative we have for the intellectual closets that we all grow up into is a nonintellectual alternative. Having had nine months of school, we spend three months in a field or factory hoeing potatoes, toting packages, learning, as we say, about Life. I have no objection to learning about Life; the best of the present ways of doing this seems to be the Peace Corps, and I would like to see half our students now heading for graduate schools take a tour of duty in the Peace Corps first. But I don't think that learning about Life in this way is a solution to the narrowness of our intellectual closets. Having learned about Life we still tend to go back into our closets when we are through. To put this in crude mathematical terms, the movement from a specialized intellectual discipline into the wilds of Life is a movement from one into an undifferentiated many. Out in the many there are no standards, or, if there are, we haven't found them yet; we haven't yet got a rational frame for Life, we *can't* concentrate on it, focus, come to grips with it; so the whole action of learning Life becomes a sort of vacation from the rigors of rationality rather than a new application of those rigors. We can learn a lot from Life and the Peace Corps, but not much that will do much for our professional closets.

No, the kind of movement I am talking about is simply from one to two. At least at the moment. One to three comes after that, then one to four. And so on. The progression is what I'm after.

For the individual, upon whom all plans for expanding our rational vision must rest, the movement from one to two could obviously involve a great many kinds of intellectual expansion. I have suggested the kinds of expansion that interest me in my own particular closet, and each of you, I am sure, can think of limited actions of a similar nature that might prove profitable in your own closets. The point would be in all cases, however, simply to double one's intellectual realm without losing control of it, losing the standards by which you have tried to run the original realm. Of course, this is not simple at all. It involves getting two educations instead of one, and also figuring out a rational relationship between the two educations.

For the cultural leader—and by cultural leader I mean simply the teacher or educator or social reformer—for the cultural leader who feels responsible for educating somebody besides himself, the movement from one to two would probably involve revising our whole present system of education, as well as our whole system of specialization out in the professions. So maybe my whole scheme is incurably utopian. Yet what I imagine is a revision, not an overturning. Again, the movement is from one to two, not from one to many or one to all. We do *not* convert courses in English to courses in general culture; we do *not* ask mathematicians to go out and seek the primordial unitive power. English remains mostly English, Math mostly Math; the atomic physicist can keep his lab. But all of them would be asked (by our cultural leader) to knock down one wall that seems to need knocking out, and thereby set about making two one.

There's nothing to it, really. To go back to the primitive instances I began with, we would not in that new world I am proposing like to give "A's" or "E's" for playing chess only. We would encourage the chess player to bake cakes too, and we would end up with a sort of cake-chess system for measuring him. Or would we? Surely not. A thousand times no. Only a committee could conceive of making *that* one out of *that* two. We must beware of what committees might do to the one-two system; otherwise a lot of money (for committees always get money) could be poured into it for no good purpose. I'm not talking about revising our hobbies and crafts. I assume that the chess player may be a mathematician at root, so he might as well develop his math talents and then perhaps, for real expansion, take a few years of Russian and Russian literature. Anyway, it is primarily his problem, not the committee's. His is the mind that needs expanding without, hopefully, any diminution of his powers of concentration in some vast bowl of cake flour. I will not presume here to make his decision for him.

Yet surely, you are perhaps thinking, I am deluded if I think of revising our educational and cultural affairs by a series of unlimited and uncontrolled individual choices in knocking down walls. I am deluded, perhaps, but not that deluded. I can imagine some relatively sensible *general* sys-

tems being devised. I can even imagine devising some myself, perhaps in another lecture. Yet here I prefer to leave all
that out and come to a stop with the individual, the individual in his closet in a world that has too many closets.

We're not going to get rid of all the closets; we
shouldn't even want to do so, for rationality itself begins
in a closet, both the best and the worst of it. But we can
perhaps enlarge some of the smallest, darkest, mustiest
closets (and thereby also reduce the total number) if we
can get the individuals in the closets dissatisfied with their
closets, wanting out. But the individual has to be dissatisfied with the "A's" he's getting in his closet as well as
the "E's," or he is still in the same closet. If only the "E"
students are dissatisfied, the closets will never change.

6

WAYS OF
MISUNDERSTANDING
POETRY

I have a big program for you. I'm going to praise spiritual drifters (with appropriate reservations); I'm going to propose a simple but revolutionary reform in the Library of Congress—elimination of the Poetry Consultant; I'm going to redefine positivism; I'm going to recommend an old movie called *Bridge on the River Kwai*. And I'm also going to talk about poetry. So although I'm not going to talk very long it will probably *seem* long. It will seem especially long when I explain, in passing, philosopher Alfred North Whitehead.

I wouldn't try such an ambitious statement if I hadn't found that ambitious statements are expected of poetry consultants. On one of my very first days here this September a reporter asked me if I thought the world was getting better or worse. I said I didn't know, which was disappointing to her. One must learn not to disappoint the press, and the press, like the rest of the world, seems to expect of its poets and poetry consultants information not available elsewhere. This is perhaps one of the basic misunderstandings about poetry, and one that the poets themselves have cultivated. I was very flattered to be asked whether the world was getting better or worse.

Which reminds me of a poem I wrote this summer, a

poem that never got past the first draft but is appropriate here:

TODAY

Today is one of those days when I wish I knew
everything, like the critics.
I need a bit of self-confidence, like the critics.
I wish I knew about Coptic, for example, and Shakti-
Yoga.
The critics I read know them, and they say so. I wish
I could say so.
I want to climb up some big publishing mountain and
wear a little skullcap and say so: I know.

Confidence, that's what I need—to know—
And would have if I came from California or New
York. Or France.
If I came from France I could say such things as, "Art
opened its eyes on itself at the time of the
Renaissance."
If I came from California I could say, "Christianity was
short-circuited by Constantine."
If I came from New York I could say anything.

I come from Minnesota.
I must get a great big book with all the critics in it
And eat it. One gets so hungry and stupid in Minnesota.

This poem, aside from its own great merits, suggests another and opposite view of the poet: far from being the
source of most worldly wisdom the poet is somebody who
writes poems because he has failed at everything else. You
may recall that Robert Frost was fond of describing the jobs
he didn't make a go at. He was a failure as a student and a
millworker and a farmer and a conchologist and a news-
paperman. He did fairly well, but only briefly and without
much staying power, at teaching school and raising poultry
(why do you suppose poultry and poetry sound so much
alike?). Furthermore, while in the poultry business (poetry

with an "l"), he displayed one of the weaknesses most commonly assigned to poets: ignorance. He wrote a piece for a magazine called *Farm-Poultry* in which he said that healthy geese are apt to roost in trees in the winter. Since geese of the garden variety, healthy or unhealthy, apparently don't do that, Frost suddenly found himself in the same boat with John Keats who had stout Cortez discovering the Pacific when he should have had stout Balboa. (You may read about Frost's further exploits with poultry—with an "l"— in an eccentric book called *Robert Frost: Farm-Poultryman*, turned out at one of the institutions Frost didn't make a go at, Dartmouth.)

It occurs to me that this view of the poet as an all-thumbs nincompoop, since it is so prevalent, might well be made into law, in which case the mysterious office I am so lucky to hold this year might actually come to perform a serious administrative function. It would issue a poetic license to each poet, and no poet would be allowed to practice in the pages of our literary journals before he had been accredited as an official fool. The interviews which I and my successors might conduct would themselves be instructive: we would ask such questions as "What is the Third Law of Thermodynamics?" or "What is a goose?" and throw the candidate out if he could tell us.

Actually this process is already in operation in many of our provinces, though it hasn't reached the Library of Congress. For example, one of the chief qualifications for admission to some of our creative writing classes and schools would seem to be an inability to pass freshman English. No more of that.

Why do we entertain these two contradictory views of poets, that they are great repositories of wisdom and that they are ignorant and ineffectual? One answer is perhaps Professor Whitehead's, that one of the views is just wrong. He had little but contempt for the values of poetic knowledge—for prophets, seers, and the like. He said, "The world's experience of professed seers has on the whole been very unfortunate. In the main they are a shady lot with a bad reputation. . . . The odds are so heavily against any particular prophet that, apart from some method of testing, perhaps it is safer to stone them, in some merciful way." I tend to sympathize with Professor Whitehead, though in doing so I am betraying my profession; that is, I am not persuaded that there is anything unique about poetic knowledge. Think of the essence of so many of our most familiar poems, which tell us that life is real and earnest, or that death conquers all, or that love is best. One doesn't need a poetry consultant to tell the country such things; and that is why I recommend that my post be abolished (after I leave, of course). Yet not all wisdom contained in poetry and poets is of such a banal sort; and rather than rejecting entirely the image of poet as prophet or wise man I would like to suggest a simple way of reconciling our apparent contradiction between wisdom and ignorance. What we need to do is to change the key words and *not* say that the poet is both ignorant and wise, but that he is frequently dissatisfied with certain conventional kinds of knowledge and peculiarly susceptible to other kinds. Thus in the case of Mr. Frost we might say, though there are many who would argue with us, that Frost made a poor student because he was suspicious of what Dartmouth and Harvard wanted him to learn, and that he made a good poet partly because of his suspicions and partly because he was open to all sorts of information from elsewhere, that is, from birches and ovenbirds and stone walls and so on. So if one were to chart Mr. Frost's knowledgeability, one would come out with a large gray patch covering a whole continent of human and natural affairs, whereas his nonpoetic academic friends would be restricted to little black spots here and there on that continent. Frost probably knew no areas of experience as well as some of his black-spot friends knew them, but there was more that he partly knew, and more that he wanted to know. He was a man who wanted to fit a lot into what I will call, for lack of a better word, his cosmology. But as thanks for his cosmological ramblings he has been called, by Yvor Winters, a spiritual drifter.

Philosopher Whitehead once said, in a quite different connection, that a cosmology should be adequate. Pithy was Whitehead. He was talking of ways of looking at the cosmos, and therefore of ways of looking at man's place and role in it; but in context he was primarily complaining of the many ways man had discovered of avoiding looking at it, particularly the way of the positivists. He was thinking primarily of scientific positivists—mostly chemists and physicists—who eschewed metaphysics on the grounds that it was not relevant to their immediate concerns, but he also had a few words of scorn for positivist humanists, that is, those who concoct great philosophies of man and society without thinking it relevant to put man in his natural and cosmological setting. Now, I am only a fourth-rate metaphysician, and you won't catch me talking at much length about the cosmos. Yet it seems to me that the phrase "a cosmology should be adequate" is one that a poet can ignore only at his peril; or in other words that positivism in all its various forms is the great modern ideological trap the poet must seek to avoid.

What is positivism? Says a dictionary:

A system of philosophy originated by Auguste Comte. It excludes from philosophy everything but the natural phenomena or properties of knowable things, together with their invariable relations of coexistence and succession, as occurring in time and space. All other types of explanation are repudiated as "theological" or "metaphysical."

Let me now convert that definition into the sense of this occasion and say that positivism is what we have here in America at almost all levels of thought and action: a philosophy of exclusion, exclusion of all knowledge that, as in intelligence circles, we do not need to know to get through the day and perform our respective duties efficiently. Specialization, departmentalization—these properly maligned components of our society—are simply products of the positivist philosophy, and we know them well; yet we do not, I think, pay enough attention to their effect upon our arts and our artists. We do not, I think, since we are all positivists by trade if not by inclination, consider sufficiently the almost insuperable problems of fostering a great art or literature in a positivist society.

But there are those who will say that I am quite wrong here, and point to the great concern constantly exhibited by modern American writers and artists for the evils of positivism around them. My opponents will cite the familiar fact about a great deal of American literature, that it expresses alienation from the American Way; and they will perhaps quote me a few thousand poems in which the limitations of our American social and spiritual vision are harped upon, poems decrying our inability to see beyond the immediacies of our restricted and regimented daily lives, to see beyond our eight—to—five commuters' jobs, our supermarkets and bathtubs and Christmases, in short, our inability to find other than immediate social and economic motivation for anything we do. One could start perhaps with T. S. Eliot's poem about the readers of the *Boston Evening Transcript:*

> The readers of the *Boston Evening Transcript*
> Sway in the wind like a field of ripe corn.

And go on to Cummings on the Cambridge ladies:

the Cambridge ladies who live in furnished souls are unbeautiful and have comfortable minds . . . they believe in Christ and Longfellow, both dead.

Or to Pound with his description of a woman dying of emotional anemia, and of artists enslaved by a botched civilization. Or to a good bit of that rather neglected poet Kenneth Fearing. Or to dozens of others. The guiding spirit here is perhaps Thoreau. Thoreau was complaining, and I certainly sympathize, against a positivism that finds irrelevant all but the conventional properties of thoughtless community living. Our modern writers follow in his footsteps and continue to bellow against the full purse and the empty spirit with the ineffectiveness we have earned the right to expect of art.

I can hear these bellowings too, of course. I have even bellowed myself, and will probably continue to do so, though, as I shall soon indicate, I think some of these bellowings are themselves positivist. Furthermore, I am persuaded that it is impossible in our society not to be positivist in some measure. Positivism, you know, is a way to money and bed and board, as well as to power. It is also a way to knowledge, knowledge within the closed circle or circuit the positivist chooses. And the kind of knowledge and control and power that positivism brings is in certain areas essential just for survival. You can't even drive downtown in Washington, for example, without being something of a positivist, that is, a being with detailed special knowledge. You have to know at what times of day what roads go which way, and how it is possible to get where you are going without ever turning left. A spiritual drifter like Frost will drift over into the sovereign State of Virginia almost every time. I sometimes wonder how many people crossing the Potomac really want to.

Now in poetry, too, a certain amount of positivist knowledge is essential for survival—survival in sophomore English or survival in the tiny literary circles that make up our poetry world. It is true, as I have already suggested, that a good many know-nothings pose as poets, persons who know little about grammar and rhetoric and less about the formal properties of traditional verse. But I do not think the real know-nothings will survive, can survive. One has to be a craftsman to be a poet—that is, a sort of specialist —and there is finally no substitute, not even pornography, for a certain minimal skill with words and forms. But that kind of skill, in modest doses, is not the kind of positivism that bothers me. Nor is it the kind of skill that, of itself, leads to power. To make the distinction I want I must refer to the movie I promised to mention, *Bridge on the River Kwai*, where two kinds of positivism are quite eloquently set before us. You may remember the movie: unlike the River Potomac the River Kwai has no bridge over it, and the problem is to make one so that the Japanese Army can drift over it. To make the bridge the Japanese employ about a battalion of British prisoners of war, mostly engineers, headed by a positivist British colonel, played by Alec Guinness, who is so interested in building bridges and observing the international rules for prisoners of war that he takes great pride in building, in record time, the best damned bridge ever made out of old bamboo. That he is building it for the enemy is not a relevant consideration for him, not at least until the very end when, with a bullet in his back, he allows his cosmology to become adequate.

The two kinds of positivism here are the technological positivism that gives the British the knowledge and power to build the bridge well and fast, and the ideological positivism that makes the colonel think that building for anybody is all right. It is the latter form of positivism, as it appears in poetry, that bothers me; we could well use more poetic engineers—and for the survival of the art we will need them—but we do seem to be building a lot of bridges for the enemy these days. The enemy is cosmological inadequacy, which is death to poetry—poetry in the largest sense of that difficult word. Let me elaborate.

I would have you consider the various ideological

views of poetry that our alienated poets put forth. I will be cavalier and assert that there are three: (1) that poetry must be pure; (2) that poetry must take man back to the simple natural world around him; and (3) that poetry must oppose, deny, subvert the whole culture and somehow salvage the individual. Obviously the three are related, but they are discussible separately, for they do tend to produce three different kinds of verse.

Pure poetry. I wish someone would mutter "art for art's sake" for me, for no poetry consultant should descend to it even though it is appropriate. There are a number of ways of characterizing poetic purity. A poem that said nothing would be pure, but I have yet to see one. A poem that said nothing capable of being generalized upon would also be pure—and lots of objective descriptions and accounts are frequently so classified, though here again I would question the possibility of real purity. And finally— here is the conventional loose use of the phrase—poems that demonstrate little or no social-political "engagement" are pure. There are lots of these, and perhaps Ezra Pound's identification of the genre with the work of Sextus Propertius may serve to characterize them. In Pound's Propertius poem Propertius is represented as hoping that he will be able to bring a few lines of verse "down from the hills unsullied." Those few lines, if he can achieve them, will last after all the emperors and generals and other men of the world, together with their works, have gone with Ozymandias into the sand. It is a familiar if constantly discredited thesis, and in our time it does not even need to be associated with the notion of the immortality of art to be espoused. The word for it now, or at least one of the words, is autotelic. A poem stands alone; it establishes its own conditions for being and can be judged only by them. Now, the autotelic principle became popular in our time in the classroom, and it was in its beginnings not so much a principle as a classroom expedient to make students actually read the poems they kept saying they were reading. I. A. Richards and then Brooks and Warren discovered that people weren't reading poetry so much as using it for a mirror; what a poem meant, what they got out of it, and what they thought of it depended entirely upon them, not upon the poem. The poem was thus merely an occasion for introspection. Or, if not that, it was an occasion for browsing about in the lives of the poets: read a bit of Shelley and then have a good cry about his death. Richards and Brooks and Warren—and of course a good many others —set about to change this softheaded view of poetry's function, and you know the results: books and books, courses and courses in close reading, in microscopic examinations of all the possible components of the world's poor struggling quatrains.

But from these researches emerged a full-blown principle about verse, that each poem is a little world with its own citizenry and streets and traffic laws and parking meters; and that anyone who enters that world—that is, any reader—is bound to live by its laws and mores. Now here, surely, is purity; here also is a most virulent positivism. I see no substantive difference between the poet or critic who adopts such a view, and the chemist or physicist Whitehead was complaining about who holes up in his laboratory and refuses to consider the metaphysical implications of his physical discoveries on the grounds that such considerations are irrelevant—or in other words refuses to believe that one needs a cosmology to live and work in one's own particular corner of the cosmos.

That's all I will say here about the ideological defects of theories of poetic purity, though obviously one could talk about them interminably. I should mention, though, briefly, a few of the practical consequences of such theories. In publishing, for example, we see a number of literary magazines, or exclusively poetry magazines, which are turned out under purity's banner. They profess to have no politics, no social or cultural views; they are merely there to print the good and the beautiful. Looking at them—and I have been looking at them for a long time—I am reminded of the center of Washington: all those monuments, all that turf, all those inscriptions, all those marble pillars and steps and busts—and not a delicatessen for miles.

Enough. Now let me turn to the second notion of poetry I wish to explode, that it must take man back to the simple natural world around him. Here also, of course, I am treading on sacred ground, even Frostian ground, and I do not wish to be misunderstood as wishing to discard the birds and the birches. I spent a wonderful month this summer with the birds and the birches in New Hampshire, and they were invigorating. I even wrote an immortal bird poem, which I will not burden you with. The first line is "One can't do much in these woods without a bird-book," and has later as one of its best lines simply a bird noise: chrrr-k, chrrr-k. So you can see that I'm in favor of birds. Furthermore I think it is true, as I have already indicated, that one of the most effective poetic ways of opposing the positivism of our society is the way of Thoreau. You may be familiar with a modern Thoreauvian book about Washington itself, called *Spring in Washington*, by Louis J. Halle, who is one of our best social-political journalists, and also, though I don't know that he has published any verse, a poet. In *Spring in Washington* he says many of the things I have been saying about positivism. For example:

It has been said before that a fundamental aim of education is to enable men to live in time and space beyond the present and the immediate. The majority of uneducated men and women appear to lead entirely somnambulistic lives, never pausing between the cradle and the grave to look up from the immediate task in hand, never raising their heads to take stock of the long past or to survey the plains and mountain ranges that surround them.

Or:

Any ape can deal with his immediate and momentary environment by instinctive reaction—as when he brushes a fly from his eyes—or even by figuring things out. That capacity to live in the universe . . . is man's alone.

Now what could be more germane to my thesis here than these remarks? Yet they arise from one intelligent man's daily confrontation with the birds and fauna down along the Potomac here. In view of such remarks how can I possibly say that poetry should not undertake to remind man of the natural world around him? Obviously I cannot. Let bird and birch poems thrive. Yet in Mr. Halle's last remark, where he distinguishes between the ape and man, I find the kernel of my complaint, a complaint not against the *expanded* vision the natural world may provide us with, but against the possible limits of that vision. For when the Thoreauvian cries out, as Mr. Halle does, against the full purse and the empty spirit, he is in danger of doing what Mr. Halle does not, in danger of proposing some simple natural life like the ape's life as a proper life, full time, for man. This is not expansion but withdrawal. Now he may do this in discouragement with man's life, as Frost does in his poem "Directive," where he recommends climbing a mountain and putting a sign up on the road behind: Closed. But to do this in the expectation that a man will be made more fully man by such an operation—this seems to me to be dangerous, except maybe on weekends. Over my library desk in the past few weeks have come a couple of dozen books of translations of primitive poetry, for example. I am not complaining about such poetry when I assert that it is very fashionable now. Some of it, particularly from Africa, may be explained away by saying that the literature of certain primitive countries is now being published for the first time because the countries are now in the world's eyes for the first time. But we also find much primitivism in our own American poetry, even in the work of very sophisticated poets. In one of Theodore Roethke's last poems, for instance, he suggests, though a bit sardonically, that he would like to become an Indian, preferably Iroquois. I like the Roethke poem, just as I like Frost's poem "Directive"—and I know that I can find in my own work plenty of withdrawal symptoms. Who does not want to withdraw after a few rounds of Washington traffic? The subject is current; the impulse is important, human, modern; so we can only be pleased that it appears in our poetry. And yet if that impulse is not balanced by other impulses— if in other words it becomes the whole blooming cosmology of a poet—then, it seems to me, it becomes a positivism in reverse, a negative positivism, still essentially positivist in being a philosophy of exclusion.

A primitivist philosophy in a nonprimitivist world is a philosophy of exclusion. When Whitehead said that a cosmology should be adequate he was being, as I understand him, deliberately relative. Such a question as "adequate in relation to what?" he would have answered culturally and historically by pointing out, shall we say, that the cosmology of a primitive Iroquois Indian would not be adequate for a modern American, Indian or not. Now, that modern American may of course be a poet—that is, one of the ignorant cusses I have already described—and in that event the cosmology adequate for him will almost surely not be Whitehead's. Yet my humility here as a poet is not unlimited; I suspect that even for me the Indian's cosmology is sure to be inadequate. To become positivist in despair and settle, not for an adequate cosmology, but for no cosmology, or a primitive cosmology, or a deliberately restricted cosmology, and then go about one's noncosmological business as if that business were in no way affected by the cosmos as it is now known to the best minds in the culture—this seems to me profoundly wrong, as well as softheaded. I am assuming in other words, with White-head, that there is at any historical moment a sort of minimal cultural-cosmological adequacy which no responsible mind can sink below and be satisfied. In sweeping and crude terms this means that adequacy in our time would have to take into account cosmologically the new occult in science, which hardly gives us back God, but hardly gives us a materialistic, mechanistic world either, and have to take into account culturally Marx, Freud, Darwin, an industrial, technological, increasingly nonrural and nonregional culture, and so on. Obviously I can't even tick off here all the diverse parts of our muddled and complicated lives that we would fit neatly together if we were all the sensible, tough-minded, cosmological poets I am suggesting that we ought to be; to do so would be as hard as telling the reporter whether the world is getting better or worse. Yet I think you can see, without my doing further ticking, the direction in which I think our poetic minds ought to move. And that direction, that right, general, impossibly difficult direction is not being moved toward in primitivist poetry.

Nor, I think, is it being moved toward by those poets who entertain the third view of poetry I mentioned, the view that poetry must oppose the culture at all costs to salvage the individual and his freedom. Most of what I have said about nature poets applies here also, but I am not talking about nature poets, I am talking about a variety of other literary anarchists. Karl Shapiro, who is one of them, and one I happen to respect, thinks this category includes all American artists. He says:

Almost to a man, American artists are in full-fledged opposition to the American Way of Life—that is, life according to Business, Politics, Journalism, Advertising, Religion, Patriotism and Morality. . . . And almost to a man, they revere the primitive America which claimed freedom of action for all men.

I don't agree. I think you will find near unanimity in the artistic community on *some* of the issues that our anarchists are constantly faced with: at the moment, for example, the issue of obscenity. The anarchists are constantly being hauled into court for obscenity, and they delight in it—some, of course, because it means fame, sales, money—but most of them because they see a principle at stake: they want to get at the moral positivists who would protect us from ourselves. The good poets of this breed Shapiro has called "authentic obscenicists," and I doubt that you will find a single committed artist in this country who would not go into court to defend his work. The freedom of all artists is crudely and blatantly at stake in such cases, the freedom, indeed the obligation, of artists to speak honestly, truly. But there is more at stake than freedom. Behind every aspiring D. H. Lawrence or Henry Miller—at least every one I am familiar with—is a theory about human nature that I do *not* think all artists share. There are all those Socialists and Communists, for example, who do not share it; what they call socialist realism is an antianarchist aesthetic of considerable import in the world; and surely there are plenty of artists on our side of the curtain who, while not social realists in the communist sense, still retain a notion of the reality of the social macrocosm in artistic endeavor. The theory of human nature which my third group of poets entertains is simple latter-day Rousseauism, with the genitals rather than the heart at the center of things, and with the human mind and all its rational accomplishments socially, scientifically, philosophically, artistically—with the human mind still relegated to a subordinate place in human affairs.

I have several angry speeches on this subject, one for instance about the word "reason" in which I point out that the very word has come to be identified with apathy and the *status quo*—or in other words with the "squares." Just so long as rationality is identified socially with the nor-

mal, the responsible, the positive, the healthy, and so on—
that is, with the administration whether the administration
be that of a college or a country—just so long will our rebels
find themselves standing for the irrational, the abnormal,
the irresponsible, the negative, the sick. Yet surely to deny
society, and to deny the mind, is simply to cultivate another
philosophy of exclusion. I won't go further into this lest I
get overwrought and lose touch with my subject here.

My subject, you remember, was "Ways of Misunderstanding Poetry." I have described, loosely, three ways, and
I have even prophesied grimly the death of poetry if the
misunderstandings are allowed to continue. I apologize for
the prophecy. Somebody is always looking for an audience
so that he can prophesy the death of poetry; meanwhile
poetry, though limping badly, does go on, and most of those
who are having anything to do with keeping it on its feet
have been guilty of one or more of the misunderstandings
I have cited. From personal experience I can report the
difficulty of avoiding these misunderstandings; I know that
I haven't consistently avoided any of them myself. There
is entirely too much to be a rebel against, to withdraw from
or to be purified of in this country of ours for most artists
to have anything but sympathy for the misunderstandings
I have cited. Perhaps then the word "misunderstanding" is
wrong, and I should substitute something else like "dismal
understanding." My title then should have been "Three
Ways of Understanding Poetry and Being Dismal."

Actually I am not sure which title is appropriate. Nor
am I sure, as I come laboriously to my message, exactly
what the message is to be. If I take the position that the
misunderstandings are really dismal understandings, then
I can hardly propose that the poets take a new look at
themselves and try to clean house; I must admit instead
that they have already looked and found the house un-
cleanable, and then acknowledge the impossibility of a reformist poetry, a poetry of engagement. Proposals for a

poetry of engagement are apt to be easy and shallow anyway; and they've been made so many times, and their sponsors have been disillusioned so many times, that one can
hardly stomach the thought of another pitiful charge on
the barricades. As Allen Tate has said somewhere, the
prospect of an effectively political poetry is like watching
Percy Shelley set a fleet of paper boats forth on the waters
of Hyde Park. No poet is going to become effectively engaged simply because he makes a New Year's resolution to
that effect or because some critic makes the resolution for
him. His reformation will take place, if it takes place at
all, only as his whole cultural being suffers some slow sea-
change away from the positivism to which he has been
bred up. For the poet is, as poet, pretty well stuck with
things as they are. He may spend fifteen hours a day in
class or in some office trying to reform the world or reform
the sentences of illiterate freshmen; but when he sits down
to his poems he is not so much a reformer as an observer,
a recorder. And if what he observes is a world in which the
creative intelligence has no role in the world's affairs, then
he will record that observation, and go to bed.

To put it differently, before the poem can be reformist
in spirit the world of the pre-poem must be reformist. It is
back there with the pre-poem, I think, where all the trouble
is. Somewhere back in the mists of the brain before the
poem emerges and gets written down is where poetry is
dying, somewhere back there where we are all potentially
poets, all potentially capable, like gods, of molding and
making sense of the world, the whole world, in which we
find ourselves. For it is back there, alas, where we all seem
to be deciding—right along with the professed poets—to be
pure, withdrawn, disengaged, softheaded. How sadly, back
there, we misrepresent the world to ourselves. The small is
big. The big is invisible. All our petty grievances and tiny
triumphs shake us to pieces; we have no emotional or intellectual resources left for the really shaking. We can't

live with the world, much less the cosmos, but just barely with our families, our bank accounts, our meager selves.

Now, if we are like this back in the pre-poem part of our culture, we can hardly expect the poem part *not* to be like this. Or so I say to myself when I would blame not the poets but the culture. I am reminded of an analogy A. J. Liebling once drew between journalism and an insane fishing industry. Perched on the shores of the ocean, he said, was a tremendous industrial fish-processing complex which unfortunately had as a source of supply only a few leaky dories manned by drunken fishermen dangling rusty hooks into the brine. The fishermen were of course the reporters, a pitiful few who had been made responsible for feeding the mighty presses of journalism. Now to transform the analogy, imagine our whole culture with all its machinery as that fish-processing plant, and imagine its workers looking wistfully out to sea for the great catch they confidently expect from the deep; and then turn your eyes seaward with them and note that the leaky dories are still the only boats out there, and now they are manned by drunken or otherwise disabled poets. My metaphor is becoming comically unwieldy, but I am trying to say that a sane culture has to have a good portion of its ablest and most intelligent members out in the boats fishing or there won't be much of a catch. Positivism keeps everybody on shore or sends them out so poorly equipped that they might as well not go out.

So at least runs my argument when I want to blame the culture and not the poets. Then I think of a poetry of engagement as nonsense. Yet at other times I think: Why hold the culture responsible?—for that is the same as having nobody responsible. One can grant that the culture has done its bit to alienate its artists—it has not only censored many of them or taken umbrage at them, but also ignored them or put them into little magazines (which is almost the same thing) while elevating to various states of social grace hordes of frauds. The culture has done its bit, but it has not done it in one simple sweeping motion, as so many of the sociological accounts of our culture's love affair with mediocrity and fraudulence suggest. What is forgotten in these accounts is that the culture is a big culture, a broad culture, perhaps best described as many cultures. It still has plenty of the kind of room in it that Whitman, for one, was always celebrating. Furthermore, its roominess is tacitly acknowledged by most of our poets themselves in their daily lives; they simply won't admit to it in their poems as they enjoy it and participate in it. Their stubbornness or blindness here is what finally leads me to accuse them of misunderstanding rather than dismal understanding, and finally to believe that the various philosophies of exclusion around us *can* be combated in some measure by the artists themselves if they will only try. Living in the woods with Thoreau, in Paris with Henry Miller, or in Yale's Hall of Graduate Studies with René Wellek—these are not the only livings available to the poet these days. And though each of these livings may be said to have its peculiar virtues, each has as well, as I have tried to indicate, limitations for which I am persuaded that the artists share at least part of the responsibility. In a way, the poets have sold themselves on their own positivism—poets from Ezra Pound to Allen Ginsberg—and now that they've got it they've also got an art that is about as central to our world as stamp collecting.

So. I have given you a polemic. Now what? What proposals for reform can I send you off home with? Would it be appropriate, for example, for me to suggest that our judiciary in its wisdom label our poets anarcho-individualists and parasites, haul them into court, and sentence them to some honest work? The Soviets did this recently with one Michael Brodsky, a poet who as an anarcho-individualist looks like Snow White compared with most of his American counterparts, but who was nonetheless found guilty of parasitism and sentenced to five years in Siberia shoveling manure. In fairness to the Soviets I should add that after a short manure term Brodsky now appears to have been let off, and to be back in circulation as a parasite. We need to remember him and his like, however, when proposing reforms. I, for example, with secret administrative yearnings in me, might, if I had the power, suddenly issue an edict prohibiting poets from writing verse, requiring them to write in the "living language" only, that is, in prose like Karl Shapiro. Or I might advocate the abandonment of literary quarterlies as now conceived and executed— "executed" is the word—or, more drastically, the abandonment of the literature departments of our colleges, on the grounds that these distinctive activities merely serve to enforce the deadly positivism of literary exclusion. I might even go about ordering poets to become physicists, journalists or—imagine—librarians. For sometimes I wish such reforms *could* be imposed on the literary world, wish there were someone in a position to impose them.

But of course nobody is in such a position. Nobody, not even a Soviet tribunal, has any effective long-term powers over literature, except maybe the power to stamp it out. For the nature of literature makes inevitable that literary reforms come from *inside* the makers of literature, not outside. Our poets and pre-poets—all those hopefully good, tough minds—have to be tolerated, even encouraged in their driftings; they have to make the decisions, do the persuading; and they have to do these things not because it would be illiberal and unAmerican for anyone to keep them from doing them—though that's a reason too—but because no outside administrator or critic has any essential authority over creation. The created thing on the page grows much the way a living thing grows in the bushes, by its own internal logic and history. Outside forces can kill it; outside forces can eventually make it modify some

of its characteristics—but that is all. Nobody has ever successfully converted a rose into a skunk cabbage, or vice
versa, by executive decree.

Which leaves us, perhaps, stuck with our skunk cabbages, at least for so long as the skunk cabbages choose to
remain as they are. And since neither skunk cabbages nor
poets are noted for their capacity to transform themselves,
we may well be in for a long era of skunk cabbages.

Yet let me suggest, in conclusion, a more optimistic
way of looking at the difficulty, by quoting a scientist who
will doubtless be astonished to hear himself thus used. He
is Cyril Stanley Smith of M.I.T. A friend of mine here in
Washington got for me a piece by Professor Smith having
to do with all sorts of structural or formal problems in
science above the level of atomic structure.* At the end of
his piece he observed that the need in science now "is for
concern with systems of greater complexity, for methods
of dealing with complicated nature as it exists"; and then
he added: "The artist has long been making meaningful
and communicable statements, if not always precise ones,
about complex things." How pleasant to have somebody
in the enemy camp think this! And how pleasant, if confusing, to hear him conclude as follows: "If new methods,
which will surely owe something to aesthetics, should enable the scientist to move into more complex fields, his
area of interest will approach that of the humanist, and
science may even once more blend smoothly into the whole
range of human activity."

Now I say this statement is confusing because, if you
have been listening to me at all you may have gotten the
impression—I certainly intended you to—that the arts, at
least as represented by much modern poetry, are hardly
blending smoothly into the whole range of human activity.

* Cyril Stanley Smith, "Structure, Substructure, and Superstructure."
Reviews of Modern Physics, XXXVI (April 1964), 524-532.

Confusing or not, Professor Smith's statement seems to me an appropriate one here, appropriate because it serves to remind us that the arts have at least a *reputation* for ranginess, and perhaps even that in past eras they have almost, on occasion, earned that reputation.

Why then can we not say that ranginess is *already* a part of the poetic organism, a now submerged part? If we do, our problem becomes not one of trying to change the organism, or trying to persuade or force the organism to change itself, but merely to encourage it to come out of the bushes and remember to *be* itself.

7
THE ARTS AND
GOVERNMENT

I've worried some about what to say to you that will make you healthy, wealthy and wise for a full academic year, and have settled on telling you everything I know. I'm going to be a pundit. A pundit is any writer who has been to Washington. I'm also going to imitate C. P. Snow, who is a superpundit, and talk about the two cultures. The two cultures for today are Washington, D.C., and Northfield, Minnesota. I'll throw in artists too, and end with a poem.

Washington first. Most of you know that our President at the moment is named Johnson and that he lives in an old white building on Pennsylvania Avenue across from the Hay-Adams Hotel. From his back windows he can look out at the Washington Monument, which has been cleaned recently, and then beyond that to the Jefferson Memorial, where the cherry trees are. The Jefferson Memorial weighs thirty-two thousand tons and has a new, free National-Park-Service brochure describing it, weighing one ounce, which I wrote.

I was Poetry Consultant at the Library of Congress and had a different view from the President's, a much longer view. I could see nearly the whole central diamond formed by the Capitol, the White House, the Lincoln Memorial, and the Jefferson Memorial, and could see out beyond the diamond too, north to the National Cathedral, where I once read a passage from Ecclesiastes in honor of Shakespeare, south across the Potomac to National Airport and the Pentagon, where I used to get lost, and west beyond

Abraham Lincoln to the residential area, Georgetown, where rich people like Kennedies and Achesons and Dulleses and poetry consultants live. There are no comparable views in Northfield.

I had trouble adjusting to the long view, having been used to looking at a few elm trees and bicycles and student petitions; so I was pretty neurotic for a few weeks. The traffic bothered me, and the location of my desk, and the bureaucratic procedures for getting a letter actually in the mails. Then there was the problem of what I was supposed to do. I had been told that I was to be consulted about the acquisition of books and manuscripts for the Library, but for weeks I couldn't even find the books and manuscripts the Library already had—thirteen million of them. And nobody brought me any books and manuscripts to be wise about. I was left dealing with a number of newspaper reporters, all of whom asked me right away what the Poetry Consultant *did*. My predecessor's reply to that— which became mine—was that the Poetry Consultant's job was to explain what the Poetry Consultant's job was. I kept saying that, but I was uneasy. It took me maybe a month to get used to not knowing what I was doing— and by then it was time for my first public lecture. Also by then I had moved my desk around and gotten aggressive in traffic and even found a book in the stacks. Also, I had met a lot of pleasant people in the Library and other agencies who didn't know what they were doing either; so I had begun to feel comfortable not knowing anything and ready for the next step in the Consultant's job: telling other people what to do. My long view was coming over me; my first lecture was called, "Three Ways of Misunderstanding Poetry." Later I moved to even bigger subjects like how bureaucrats can cope with artists, how artists can cope with bureaucrats, why English teachers need to be reeducated, and architects destroyed—and how to bring peace to the world.

There were a few other poets in Washington, though it isn't a poet's town. One of them was Paul Goodman, an anarchist whom some of you have read or heard (he came to Carleton a few years back on the American Studies Program, talking about city planning; he's an old hand at telling people what to do). Last March a meeting was held at the Library of Congress about the arts in government; Goodman came to it in tennis shoes and a moth-eaten sweater and a pipe. When I proposed that something artistic be done to improve bureaucratic prose, he pointed out that this would be impossible because it would involve making bureaucratic prose say something. Saying something, he said, was what bureaucratic prose was designed to prevent. Obviously, Goodman doesn't work for the government; he's just an anarchist dismayed by government who has attached himself to a private agency that sits in the neighborhood of government and complains. The Poetry Consultant's job is a little like his—that is, the Consultant is mostly just in the neighborhood (he is not on the public payroll)—so he can choose to be anarchist too, if he likes that sort of thing.

He's not as free as Goodman. He does have obligations to the Library, and his role is so public that he can get the Library in trouble. But he wouldn't be filling his post properly if he just settled in to be a bureaucrat. He is supposed to be a sort of court fool—an anarchist within the system.

Now you can see that my thesis is shaping up. I'm setting up some familiar alternatives. To be or not to be an anarchist. To be or not to be part of the system. To be free or responsible, permissive or disciplinary. To be a nightingale or an ant—and so on. You know where the modern American poet is reputed to stand on such matters; he has, collectively, a reputation that makes it hard for him to be recognized as a poet at all if he is not an anarchist verbally, intellectually, socially and—if a teacher—pedagogically. In some quarters he is expected to make a *career* of denying the going systems, denying plebeian assumptions about what is mannerly and moral and responsible, about what is healthy and profitable and useful, and about what is honest and true. One can make a good case for saying that the mainstream of our poetry is out of the mainstream. The poet—as collectively thought of—is a rebel against old literary forms and old pieties, against patriots and prudes, against bourgeois sweetness and light, and against bureaucratic darkness and red tape. Melville described this rebelliousness as a striking through the mask, and we've been stuck with it since. The poet—that collective poet—has assumed that his own private judgment is superior to the judgment of his neighbors and that the publication of his tiny verses is more important finally than the dissemination of train-loads of textbooks, scholarly monographs, or government pamphlets. And for his troubles as a minority hero he's been well rewarded, except in the sales of books. He's lived to see many of his private judgments against his society confirmed by the stupidity and blindness of the society. He's been able to watch the society keep failing to provide its citizenry with the full life, the relevant life, the spiritually and physically rewarding life—keep failing, I mean, to provide a life of which the poet would approve.

To be rewarded by being right is the best kind of reward. It's nice to find out what's wrong with someone who has made a go in the world, and what's wrong with the world he has made a go in. We can go right back to Hamlet, say, and see what satisfaction Hamlet got out of discovering the villainy of Claudius, the rottenness of Denmark. And I could play Hamlet right here now—as probably many of you could—and pitch in with a number of private examples of how money or prestige or power has gotten in the wrong hands, has been misused, and has led to public injustice, private discontent. In fact, in the arts these findings are commonplace. There's hardly a poet or novelist or musician or painter but is amazed if some big award like the National Book Award or the Pulitzer Prize actually reaches someone he admires. That the system rewards the wrong people, that the wrong people control the system—and that ultimately all the real rewards of life, whatever they are, must be found in some hole in the wall outside the system—these have become first principles in the minds of a whole community of artists.

I don't think I need to credit or discredit these principles to observe that Washington is an interesting place in which to watch the principles at work, at work in conflict with the greatest system of all, the Federal Government. Especially from the detached office of the Poetry Consultant. The Consultantship is a Washington freak. It came into being in its present form right after the war when various forces against the system stormed the Library and captured one office up on the third floor in front. They have held on since, through the regimes of maybe fifteen Consultants, and, while many of the Consultants have been good system men, the office has preserved a remarkable purity, or antisystem flavor. I'm not revolutionary myself—and in a minute I'll tell you of a couple of occasions when I prostituted myself for the system—but the Library officials with whom I dealt assumed from past experience that I would be troublesome, and sometimes they were positively embarrassed when they had to ask me to be systematic, or friendly with system forces. I remember, for example, a friend of mine at the Library suggesting, as if he were asking me to take a salary cut, that I have lunch with a best-selling novelist who happened to be working at the Library. He knew that poets, respectable poets, normally had no truck with Book-of-the-Month-Club people. I also remember how hard my associates worked to protect me from system representatives like American Legion poets and State poets and lovely-tree poets and moral-uplift poets; sometimes I felt like an invalid whose nurses think he'll collapse if he learns what's *really* going on out in the hall.

Yet there the Consultant is. And there, off and on in our big new culture era, are representatives of all the other arts too. Most of you know that art suddenly hit Washington all of a heap during the Kennedy Administration. There were great receptions for artists at the White House and elsewhere, with a great deal of attendant publicity. Committees were formed; programs were projected; and a kind of arts czar was appointed, August Heckscher, who eventually produced a report that has really established Washington's "line" toward the arts right up to now. The report advocated increasing governmental "responsibility for the arts," noted the need for keeping the arts "under survey," and celebrated the importance of the arts in improving, promoting, sustaining our culture, especially our culture overseas. In it the bad boy of the culture, art, was suddenly put at the head of the class, but no mention at all was made of his being a bad boy. This oversight was more than compensated for by making the boy a charity case. The vague and wonderful things that art can be imagined to do for a culture were made the occasion for proposing that government get in the business of subsidizing artists—but not of hiring them.

It was in this context that plans for the Kennedy Memorial for the Performing Arts in Washington were devised, that the new governmental arts foundation was created, that dozens of artists were invited to President Johnson's Inaugural (and carted around in buses labeled "Cultural Leaders"), and that an Arts Festival was held at the White House this last June in honor of prominent national patrons of art. So it is in this context that the subject of the artist as rebel—at least as rebel against big government—needs to be discussed. How does the artist retain

his integrity when being patronized by the system? And
how do the systematizers like being bitten by their own
charity cases?

If you listen to artists you will hear various expressions
of doubt—not about their capacity to accept patronage
(artists have many rationales for being unscrupulous about
money)—but about the capacity of any system or system
representative to take an artist seriously. But if you listen
to the system men you are apt to find them evading the
bad-boy side entirely and talking, as Heckscher did, about
the misty role of art in the culture. When I went to Washington I got a full dose right away of the system men's
evasions. I was constantly being asked to sell creativity,
while being enjoined against being political. The line I
took here was that bureaucrats all wanted creativity to begin
at 8:30 in the evening, or at least after working hours. The
image of the artist—and he was preferably from the performing arts—the artist as a blithe spirit somehow bringing
new strength and vigor to the society without at the same
time getting soiled by, or soiling, the mundane daily affairs
of the society—this was the prevalent image, and as my
year went on down there, I saw more and more instances
of how important that image was, and of how hard the system men worked to hang on to it—sometimes blindly and
sometimes with intelligence and admirable good faith. Let
me give you two cases.

First there was the case of the Park Service pamphlet
for the Jefferson Memorial, which I've mentioned. The
publications section of the Park Service conducts a big and
thoroughly bureaucratic operation, but it has many energetic people working for it who like to imagine themselves
back in the thirties harnessing artists, as the WPA did, to
bureaucratic jobs. I was pleased to find them coming around
to consult me, and I suggested that they start a program
to get writers from outside the Park Service to write *and
sign* some Park-Service pamphlets. (This signing is im-

portant. Present conventions make government prose anonymous—only the department head's name normally appears, in this case Secretary Udall's). I ended up writing the Jefferson piece as an experiment, and after it was finished I was surprised to see how much importance the publications people attached to getting it up through channels with all its minor individualism still intact. We went over the piece a few times together—I remember striking out a witty line about the stupidity of congressmen—and we decided that though it was stylistically revolutionary (it had a few jokes in it and small ironies), and though it was critical of the original planning for the Memorial, in the way that a government publication is not supposed to be, not a word should be changed. The author's integrity should be insisted on against the red pencils of the bureaucrats up above.

Now this was a tempest in a teapot. The piece was innocuous. But as the proceedings went on, I began to share the publication people's excitement in trying to crack the system sociably from inside—I'd have been willing to make a number of other changes they decided I shouldn't make, to guarantee the piece's passage. I don't know what will come of the experiment, but I went away persuaded that we had a glimpse of what can and cannot be done to bring together government and art.

The other instance is larger, probably less happy. I doubt that many of you know what 1965 is: it is ICY, International Cooperation Year. You wouldn't know it, would you? Anyway, last June when I was involved with it, there were eighty or more American committees churning out proposals for international cooperation in every possible field—the proposals all to be dumped on the President's desk. Half of the committees were in the "public sector," half in the private. For a couple of months I served on the public-sector "Committee for Culture and Intellectual Exchange," and we would meet every couple of weeks, some-

times alone and sometimes with our private-sector counter-
part. What did we talk about?—about more books in more
places, about a reverse Peace Corps, about international arts
festivals, about international conferences on natural beauty,
or conferences about racial, religious, and ethnic relations
in the modern world. All that and much more, including
the problems of how to get it all on the President's desk.
I sat fairly quiet and made only one significant proposal—
a proposal for a series of dialogues on the aesthetic split between East and West, that is, between socialist realism and
whatever it is that we have, maybe what the Soviets call
the cult of the individual—I sat fairly quiet until at one
point the promoters among us tentatively began to plan an
advertising campaign for ICY, a beating of drums for a
production not even on the boards yet. Then I objected,
for two reasons. First, I felt that any exclusively American
promotion of ICY at this point would make the ICY look
like just another State Department front (this was a feeling State Department people shared—the promotional sug-
gestions came from the private sector). Secondly—and I suppose this is my artist's reason—I felt that a few more empty
abstractions for publicity purposes about the international
importance of art in five colors in the *Saturday Evening
Post,* and I'd throw up.

I'm out of touch now. I don't know where ICY went.
But for my purposes here the results of the Committee's
activity are less important than the activity itself. What
were we doing at those meetings? Were we hopefully leading art into the *service* of a great social goal—that is, international understanding? (That's after all a pleasant utopian
thought.) Or were we proposing to *exploit* art for that high
purpose? The line between service and exploitation is hard
to draw, but the connotations of the two words are im-
portantly different; and I think it is of some national significance which word Washington—now that it has discovered art—comes to side with.

Washington is a unique American city in relation to the
notion of service, a point I can make only by digressing a
moment. A good deal of the traditional morality of our
culture is bound up with the happy meanings of service—
service to state or country, service to a church, service to a
family or to some small paternalistic social order. Shakespeare rings all the changes on service, but is probably at
his best on it in *King Lear*. There Cordelia, Kent, and a
few others are the traditionalists; Edmund, on the other
hand, is the new man for whom the connotations of the
word "service" are servility and exploitation—and of course
he will have none of it. Service, the traditional notion, goes
along pretty well in English literature and elsewhere,
though, despite Edmund, until the revolutionary late-
eighteenth century, when the old servers take over and run
into difficulties finding masters worth serving. From then
on service—the traditional notion—is in trouble, and for
every Cordelia who thinks of service in the happy traditional sense of rendering spiritual obedience to an "x," or
ministering to the wants or well-being of an "x," or regulat-
ing one's conduct in accordance with the spirit, fashion
and demands of an "x"—for every Cordelia who conceives
herself to be merely acting according to her bond, there is
an Edmund who thinks of service as subservience, slavery.
I think it is safe to say that now there are more Edmunds
than Cordelias, at least in our country; and though the
Edmunds are apt to be idealistic Edmunds (they are apt to
look like Henry David Thoreau), still their contempt for
service is evident in most phases of their conduct. The point
about service in the old sense is that it was never that wonderful American thing, self-service. There was always a
clearly visible, concrete "x" *other* than the self to serve.
Thoreau and others managed to destroy that "x"—many of
them had good reasons but they nonetheless destroyed it—
they destroyed the "x" and substituted for it, if they felt
they needed to substitute anything other than self, an

abstraction like the General Good or the Oversoul or—the current terms—Freedom, Integration, Peace.

End of digression (though obviously there is no end to it). Back to Washington. The unique thing about Washington is that in a country heavily committed to self-service, Washington retains a strong traditional sense of service even though the entity being served, the "x," is mostly a newfangled untraditional governmental thing. Washington is mighty confused on the subject, though, as it should be. On the one hand it has the inclination to let the new world of self-service in—so it sends all sorts of anarchic American artists abroad to represent us, and wants to encourage individuality, creativity, and so on—and on the other it has its channels, its many devices for subordination of self in the service of governmental "x's." Nor are these channels, these devices for self-subordination, merely dead, mechanical things. I am not talking now about the mechanics of Washington but its spirit, a spirit of selflessness and service in the old sense that remains very strong despite the McCarthies and Bobby Bakers and miscellaneous poetry consultants.

I was impressed by that spirit and by the hundreds of hard-working civil servants who whizzed off every day to sometimes humdrum, sometimes interesting, but always frustrating jobs, not well paid, to which they really do dedicate themselves. I came around to thinking that though sometimes the high-level decisions were obnoxious, and though some of the low-level activities were useless and boring, our civil servantry as a whole displayed a human dignity that any artist worth his salt, no matter how jealous of his individualism, could only come to admire. But my impressions are not important. My point is simply sociological: Washington is by its nature a service town—imagine a town devoted entirely to administration; you think you have it bad!—and being a service town it might well fall apart if it got into the hands of the Edmunds of

America, good or bad Edmunds. But if it is to administer to an Edmund country it must obviously draw upon Edmunds for some of its talent and, of course, administer to Edmunds. A real predicament. It is this predicament that makes Washington's dealings with artists tricky. Whenever President Johnson invites a painter or musician to the White House, whenever the State Department ships a poet off to Pakistan, or whenever various agencies collaborate on a big cultural production like the ICY affair I mentioned, one can look at the act in two ways: that is, one can say that the artists in question are simply being wooed to join in a traditional service effort; *or* one can say, in the spirit of Edmund, that they are being picked off like plums for the market; they are being exploited by just another self-interested party for their names and works (this is why I worried about the ICY's cultural affairs in the hands of the National Advertising Council).

When the poet Robert Lowell publicly declined his invitation to the White House arts festival last June, he was obviously, though troubled about it, thinking "exploitation." I've forgotten his phrase—something about fearing to make "subtle commitments" (in this case, commitments to our war in Vietnam) if he were to accept—but whatever the phrase he clearly had the problem I'm talking about in mind. It's a big problem. An Edmund will decide it as Lowell did; a Cordelia may decide it as Ralph Ellison did (he went to the Festival, and didn't complain). And between the two, Washington keeps being shaken to the roots. What happens to my Jefferson pamphlet or even to ICY and the new art foundation—these are minor, peripheral matters in the great Washington crush—but the problem they engender is not peripheral.

One can argue of course that to patronize art as the present government programs do is a way to *avoid* exploiting art. One gives the artist money or artistic opportunity or a pass to the White House lawn without demanding anything of him in return—hence no exploitation. But if the patron's commitment is not more than a commitment of money and facilities—that is, if there is no substantial intellectual or spiritual link between the patron and what he is patronizing, then the chances that the art will be exploited are great. Then the art can become, as we all know, merely a pretentious showcase for Veblen's leisure class, or, in the case of Washington, merely a showcase for democracy, vague high-mindedness, what-all. So although the dangers of exploitation of artists asked to *serve* are also great—the example of the Soviets is the commonly cited case in our time—I see no way to avoid the conclusion that an engaged artist, an involved artist, a serving, functioning artist is potentially the least exploited artist. He has been let in; he is a member of, not just a performer for, his culture.

Washington is not yet ready to admit artists to membership, I'm afraid. All its present programs largely stem from the Heckscher document I mentioned; they all tend to make art eligible for patronage and therefore *out* of service. But it would be wrong to think that Washington is to blame; the general climate for art in this country does not encourage the service notion—here Washington necessarily takes its cue from the provinces, and, if anything, the provinces are less ready to get art into the working day than is Washington. I paraded around Washington last spring with a small program of my own; like a Marxist I was trying to sell what I called the "useful arts"; and I was encouraged by the interest, maybe academic, that I found for the program. As I said earlier I held a couple of meetings in my ivory tower at the Library—which persons from various agencies attended—and at these I thought I had quite a bit of support for planting writers and designers around in the bureacracy like cherry trees and asking them to serve. Of course I wore my example of the Thomas Jefferson brochure to a frazzle, for it was the only artistic fact

I had as evidence in a sea of high resolutions; but I got the impression that the Department of Agriculture was as ripe as the Park Service for, say, a consultant in prose or a consultant in design, that the Smithsonian could readily keep half a dozen artists in residence and working, and that even HEW might bite if the artists suggested to them also looked, on a dark night, a bit like educators. I should also mention that I had a short romance with NASA, the space agency, which oddly already has an arts program: it sends prominent painters down to Cape Kennedy to watch a few blast-offs and possibly to paint space. So I optimistically concluded that though the present arts programs seem to exclude usefulness and service for art, there is hardly a governmental agency in Washington without secret artistic yearnings waiting to be satisfied, and that to satisfy them a new program with the word "service" in capital letters in it was the ticket. The big catch was: Where were the artists to fill out the program? That is, where were the Edmunds willing to give up some of their Edmundness to work for, or at least within, the system?

This brings me by a long route to Northfield, good Edmund country. Or maybe I should say Thoreau country, Thoreau the good Edmund. Northfield is a town with not one but two presidents as well as a mayor (unlike Washington, Northfield has home rule). Each of our two presidents is surrounded by a large brain trust with long views. A member of the trusts can look out through clear air for miles and see nothing but brains. There is no department of agriculture or labor, there is no congress, there are no embassies, no heavy memorials, no cherry trees. There are not even any traffic lights. So although there are two systems—the three-three and the four-four-one—Northfield is not strong on systems, at least comparatively. It is out on the outer edge of systems, in what might be called system-testing country. Some of the brains here are very systematic indeed, and some of them have never even learned to

set an alarm clock. In the center of the whole complex
are a pool hall, a liquor store and a movie house; on the
fringes is corn, soon snow.

I'm not going to say much about Northfield, but what
I have to say can be broached with a question that a local
reporter asked my wife when we got back a few weeks ago.
He wanted to know if she thought there was anything in
Washington that Northfield could incorporate. She didn't
answer, but she and I have been mulling it over since. Now
you can. We don't need the Pentagon. Nor the new Sam
Rayburn building. Nor the little statue to Faith, Hope,
Charity, and Temperance on Pennsylvania Avenue. Nor do
we need, I think—my political remark for the day—to worry
as much as we do about our administrative *system*. Like
everyone here, I can think of lots of changes I would like
to make, and I've always felt it my duty to undermine the
place a bit every year. But anyone coming from a big systems center like Washington can only be impressed by the
relative freedom from system here. Our systems problems
are not central, or not as they are in Washington. To the
visitor from Washington, Northfield looks like Walden
Pond.

But of course it is not Walden Pond; and its deceptive Walden-Pond look may be our trouble. Not only does
the Internal Revenue Service get up this way, but the farm
subsidies do too, and there's a public school system, a road
system, a postal system, a banking system, telephone and
utilities systems, a curriculum, and so on. It's obvious that
the most anarchic members of this community are systems
men to a degree whether they think so or not. The platitudes about our little colleges—that thank God they are
still free of the systems—is just wrong, except relatively.
The freedom you are systematically scheduled to enjoy
this year is no absolute, any more than the system our civil
servants are chained to in the Capital is an absolute. These

categorical opposites are nonsense, and nobody can live sensibly or happily in either place with them.

I mean simply, as far as Northfield is concerned, that it doesn't follow that because we are in the mesh of modern systems we are in a terrible mesh. In fact I'm trying not to evaluate the mesh at all, just get at the necessity of acknowledging it, acknowledging it as a *presence*. The "is-ness" is what I'm talking about. Washington senses that "is-ness" of course; it can't avoid doing so. But I don't see how Northfield, or Carleton, can either.

Back to artists. Artists, like teachers and students, have to contend all the time with what might be called the pre-system self. I mean they're stuck with it—so it is no wonder that they get to be the way they are about systems. But an artist in Northfield or Washington—an artist anyplace in this system country—can hardly ignore what *is*, and if he is any sort of good modern realist he knows it, at least theoretically. But he can be a master of self-deception when it comes to defining the "is" and placing himself in relation to it. Take a writer, say, with seven children in the public schools and a thoroughly socialized Westinghouse icebox in his kitchen and a big group retirement plan for his old age in his files, carrying a driver's license with him—that is, a permit from his society to drive—and perhaps a Shell credit card as he drives all over the country on the new federal roads—take this writer, this highly socially engaged writer who would die in thirty-six hours on the desert island his mind unfortunately lives on, take this writer and ask him if he wants to work for the system. More than likely he will suddenly squat down like a zen Buddhist and wait sanctimoniously for what is called "satori." At the very least he will say that an artist who traffics with the system is a whore.

He will say this because he fears for his freedom, his creativity, his independence of thought and action—those big virtues. He knows the implications of the acceptance of systems, intellectual and social, and so he throws the systems away. As if he could.

That "as if" is no good. He can't live with himself very long *as if* he were free. He must know the dimensions and limits of his freedom—that is, his *given* relationships to the systems he is a part of—or he's an ignorant man.

I'm done with the preaching part now. If you meet me on the street later, you'll hear me qualifying what I've said, showing off my own anarchic impulses, and vacillating between the positions of Edmund and Cordelia—but I'm going to end now as I threatened to, by reading a poem. I hope it will suggest how I personally get bogged down as a writer when I try to cope with the concurrent demands of self and system. Its a discursive poem—I mean talky, meditative, prosaic. The scene is an artists' colony in New Hampshire where I've now spent two summers and where, I know, the self gets a real workout. The self gets pushed away in a little studio, all alone in the woods, with nothing but a blank wall and a few birds and trees to look at (the blank wall plays an important part in the poem). The poem is in the form of a letter, and the letter is to God, and it is very long—several minutes even.

Dear God

Though I don't believe in you, I've decided to write you.
Do with my words what you will—do you have a file?—
But don't imagine me sitting down here pining away for an answer.
It's not that kind of letter,
But a common poetic trick you would know about, if you kept up,
For talking at large to one's self without feeling ill.
A number of other poets have tried such things, whose names I won't mention,
And not one of them would have been happy with your reply.
Nor I.

So don't worry, I'll do the worrying, about you, and art, and
    man,
Especially man. You fly your atoms.

Your sun is coming out now, after a drab dawn.
My dog is out on the steps eating a soldier (plastic).
I feel headachy, constipated, mildly depressed, dull.
As usual I'm at my desk looking north at a blank wall
For art's sake, art being what many walls and other
    uninterrupted densities
Are for: to turn the eyes back in boredom to the more or less
    boring self
Where the treasure, if there's a treasure, lies, if it hasn't been
    stolen,
Waiting for Tom Sawyer, who doesn't exist,
To come along with a chart with an "x" on it
And dig up. Out past the wall
Is a pretty thick stand of pines which makes a good wall, too.
My acres are jammed with artists, most of them younger,
Armed with palettes and Steinways, looking at walls.
I wish them good hunting, I envy them some, I suppose I'd
    trade walls
Or selves with any of them, in a minute, if asked,
So I could write a big lovely ode or sonata to treasurable me.
Not asked, I must sit here, self-old, and try to take solace
From the knowledge that at least my wall has little of me left
    behind it.

One can't make an easy living exploring the self—that's for
    sure—
Which may be the reason such explorations enchant us so
    much,
Too much. We take a big healthy hunk of artist
Who likes to talk, drink, make love, play tennis
And so on, and what do we tell him? We make him a patient.
We say: you need to be alone, desperately, you need privacy.
Take a month, take two, three, get away someplace—
New Hampshire's nice—
Get away and get to it: write, paint, sculpt, create, create.
And of course he does get to it, like mad. Who wouldn't? The
    woods are lovely,

Dark, deep, just dandy in every respect except that the life in
them
Becomes a kind of irrelevance or aside.
The patient is well, perhaps even happy, but just barely
breathing.
He's art, all art, and his art is all art, and shows it.
Sometimes, fed up, he thinks he'd be better off, though he
wouldn't be,
If he set up shop in the middle of some city sidewalk.
At least he'd be looking at people, other people. The self gets
tiresome,

As your son and a number of other religious leaders have
pointed out.
I should join with them perhaps, sign the dotted line, be part
of a lump,
Piously anonymous, selfless, sweet, sacrificial, forgiving—and
not writing.
For I wouldn't write then, not a bit. Art, at least American art
—and this is the curse on it—
Derives its force mostly from those who'd be gods on their own.
We're lucky of course, terribly lucky to be so well fixed
That playing at god isn't necessarily mad, paranoid.
Yet perhaps we'd be luckier less lucky. I don't mean salt mines.
I don't mean schools of hard knocks, every poet-boy a paper
route
(Though I must say that as I get older and *they* get younger,
They keep looking softer and softer to me, more parasitic).
What I mean is that if there had been no woods, no ready
refuge
For our artists—if the chance for seclusion, separation, removal
had never been dangled—
Then we wouldn't be stuck with our god-myth, our art would
be different.
We'd be happily adjusted little social slaves busily creating
Lovely works of engagement (like a good slave should) rather
than woods work.

So here I am plumping for slavery? Well, poor thing,
She's had a bad press lately. The press is free, except when it's
tied up.

So are students and dogs. I'm free, we're all free, except mostly,
Free not to go to church, free to vote for Johnson,
Free to smoke (though they're working on that), free to write
  naughty words—
So we hate slavery.
But the rhythm of things is slave, good or bad, but slave.
An artist without the rhythm, trapped in his free woods,
Is a fortunate lost soul in an absolutely top-notch, first-class,
  free Siberia,
With the Constitution and the Supreme Court slaving overtime
  to keep him there,
And the big foundations spending all sorts of money to keep
  him there,
Keep him off the rhythmical beat for his own sweet sake who
  most needs the beat,
In the name of freedom. Enough. I can hear forty-seven
  Congressmen
Asking me cuttingly if I'd live in the real Siberia, by choice.
Of course not, I can't speak the language, I don't know a soul
  there,
I couldn't get my car repaired and, darling, you know how cold
  it gets.

Cold, cold for the self: slavery. But many, many the slave places
  south of Siberia,
And many the cold ways to those cold places—war, for example.
There's a war bumbling near right now, as always—*the* war?
And can the self keep clear?
It can sit in, sit down, lie in, lie down, march in front of the
  White House, make speeches;
But when the war comes if it comes, with the solemn Pentagon
Faces crowding the papers like a locust plague,
And everyone climbing in khaki to defend to the death
The self from its unredeemable enemies in our nearly eternal
  horse opera,
Then—tootle tootle bang pop—
The ships, troops, guns, bombs, savings bonds and casualties
  take over and darken the landscape,
And not the tiniest self in the smallest, artiest, most New
  Hampshirean hole
Can keep clear. Self in a war?
There's vanity just thinking it.

And as for that breezy, happy, pastoral alternative, peace,
Imagine a bright blue day,
A justice day, a rights day, a day when a bruised peach would
   go to court,
And the patrons of art are out on the streets commissioning
Portraits for upstairs halls, plays for long Riviera yacht trips,
While Shakespeare fans out alarmingly from Central Park,
And General Motors buys a controlling interest in the
   Association of Literary Magazines of America—
Imagine that blue, blue day, and the self, with its wall,
Staring all day at the blankness, then tearing up paper,
Blackening canvasses, fiendishly chopping up granite
In sheer impotence—
Imagine it grinding home in your loveliest sunset
To kick the dog in the yard and blow down the pretty home,
   whoof,
With the children inside at TV and the wife in the kitchen,
Pow, and have a quick six drinks and rage off to a bad movie
To return again, again to clamber all lonely,
Shhh, into its bed where it falls asleep reading a road map.

You're really quite lucky, you know, not to exist.
If you did I would hold you responsible for these ambiguities
In what might have been a nice, clean, well-lighted place
With the self and freedom trumpeting out of the juke box at
   two,
And society, slavery, responsibility at three, round the clock,
A pleasing alternation peacefully handled—no factions,
   disputes,
Everyone awfully polite, slave and anarchist dancing. As things
   stand,
When your moon goes over, and your sun, and the shelf items
   click into position—
Bee, sunflower, leaf, cloud, woodchuck—
The self in its freedom can slave at its own absurdities
At such depths and in such imperial darkness—Liberty Hall!—
As any old Egyptian slavemaster would gawk at. Or you for that
   matter.

Enough. I'll write a book later. It's too muggy now.
All the bits and pieces of nature that in a better world than this
   one would be yours

Are indefinite at the edges. I can see no artists at all, but I
    know that they're out there,
Struggling against the heat and the walls to retain their
    integrity,
Which some of them know and some of them don't know that
    they can't possibly keep.
But going hard at it anyway, as I am.
I don't know what else to tell you. I look all around me, and
    inside,
And am shamed mostly,
Not by country or freedom, not by Congressmen
(Them I'll put in the book),
But by the spectacle of the self, the pompous self,
The minuscule godlet strutting behind the wall,
And with unmitigated gall
Surviving, thriving, bragging, beating his chest, despite all.
Dear God, could you bless him?

8

ON GRADUATE TRAINING
IN ENGLISH, YET

*[An address to English teachers at a meeting of the
Modern Language Association]*

OF COURSE WE all know that we teach the best that man
has known and thought. We realize that if only our students
could come to know our potful—come to know it as well
as we fortunate ones know it—all would be well. Our chief
trouble is with the other potfuls. Not all of them are bad,
but all of them are distracting. If only they would go away.

The nice thing about graduate training in English is
that it helps them go away. In graduate school we can
study our potful to the bottom, keep busy, and in the
process defend civilization genteely against the Huns. This
is the good life.

But sometimes some of us have little twinges while
thinking about this good life, either as we see it in the
graduate schools or as we see it later out in the big world
of the classroom. While we are plowing through *Titus
Andronicus* or "The Vanity of Human Wishes" or even
"The Waste Land," we are apt to say, "Oh, God, again?"
—not out loud of course—and entertain the destructive
thought that perhaps these are not such hot instances of
the best that man has known and thought after all. Can
it be that we are not always obeying our great cultural
mentor's injunction to see the object as in itself it really is?

I am an impostor (I have no graduate degree, none),
and so I have perhaps had more small doubts like these

than most of you here. Just a month ago I was trapped in southwestern Virginia answering the question, "Should English departments be destroyed?" I like the tone or texture of that question, and would be glad to have you trap me into coming to your school to answer it. Meanwhile, however, I must tell you what to do with our graduate schools.

But not too fast. I must digress right away and describe some eccentric thoughts I have been having recently about rhetoric, and some eccentric thoughts a friend, Howard Nemerov, has been having independently about the novel. I'll start with Nemerov.

Nemerov's most recent book, *Journal of the Fictive Life,* begins with some observations by a fictional novelist about novels and the presuppositions that lead to novels:

The novel, then, was a way of constructing a certain feeling of reality, rather than a reality, by means of formal presuppositions about life, especially the one which claimed that life was a story. . . .

So, this novelist then observes, one should go get one's self a story and then, to make it realistic, add detail. How tiresome, especially if one has already written a story. "To do all that again," the novelist reflects cynically, "describe the furniture, provide these people with different noses." In only a few pages he manages to persuade himself that he doesn't want to write a novel at all:

In middle life, you perceive as though suddenly what was always there to be perceived, that all the stories are only stories. Beyond the stories, beneath them, outside the area taken account of by stories, there are the sickbed, the suffering, the hopeless struggle, the grave. It makes the stories look like hypocrisy, and the vision is so terrible that one becomes humbly grateful for the hypocrisy.

These thoughts lead Nemerov to abandon his mask as fictional novelist and become simply Nemerov (though Nemerov is never simple), and then to speculate about why he personally wrote novels in the first place. He finds that his motives have been all mixed up with money and success and doing the right thing:

For a Jewish Puritan of the middle class, the novel is serious, the novel is work, the novel is conscientious application—why, the novel is practically the retail business all over again.

On the other hand, he notes,

Poetry is exalted pleasure, and in the world of my childhood and adolescence, pleasure is primarily known as something that has to be paid for. A characteristic metaphor for this division has occurred to me many times: the novel is marriage. Poetry is infidelity.

I will abandon Nemerov at this point, though I have taken you only to page twenty of his remarkable book, and switch over to my own separate thoughts about rhetoric, which turned out also to be referrable to the marriage-infidelity metaphor. With a psychologist colleague at Carleton, John Bare, I have been looking for a way of pushing Freshman Rhetoric—or at least some of the problems of Freshman Rhetoric—over into other departments of the college. This is a utopian venture in team teaching that I won't describe here, just telling you that it has led me into the thick of the search for a "new rhetoric." The search started when my colleague and I discovered again what every composition teacher discovers every year, that his students seldom look at what they are asked to describe. You ask the student, "What do you see?"—as Walker Gibson does in his textbook *Seeing and Writing*—and instead of answering the question the student tells you what he thinks or what he thinks he thinks. The primary step, of looking, keeps getting left out. Very well. Get the primary step back in. Nothing to it.

So we went about getting the primary step back in, trying to devise a few exercises in what they were looking at in Psych 10: commonplace exercises in the recording of perception. And after a bit of that, we moved on to other rhetorical problems such as What Is Rhetoric Anyway?— and one day I was hard at the business of summarizing for them the ingredients of Aristotelian rhetoric when I realized that Aristotelian rhetoric left out the primary step too.

I shouldn't say quite that. Induction is there, of course, and my scholarly friends tell me that Aristotle prescribed ten times the induction per square enthymeme that his Renaissance successors did; but it is there in very incomplete form. Something is given us right at the start, something we are expected to advocate with marvelous eloquence *rather than* investigate. Why else would Aristotle say, for example, that "when decisions are not made as they should be, the speakers with the right on their side have only themselves to thank for the outcome." The speaker's job, that is, is to sell the right, not determine it; the right has somehow already been determined.

Now you may protest, hoping to keep ultimate questions out of this, that it is of the nature of rhetoric that it addresses itself to expression rather than investigation. The investigation is a necessary prelude to the expression (and Aristotle urges it upon us), but it remains a separate subject. My ignorant answer here is that the Greeks didn't *have* a separate subject to resort to, except dialectic, which is not at all the kind of investigating I am talking about. They had a very primitive notion of the investigatory mode, a notion that we continue to entertain by still preaching the classical rhetoric.

But I don't want to get tangled up in this big problem here. I prefer to save my most damaging remarks about

Aristotle for audiences less learned than this one. All I am trying to get at is that this last term, in trying to get my students to tell me where and how in their investigations they arrived at the stuff they were rhetorically giving me, I discovered that mostly they didn't know. Not only that, I discovered that the character of what they thought they knew tended to change, like the revolving lights at burlesque shows, as the rhetorical demands they faced changed. They were getting their cues about the "right" from me or from some other audience rather than from their own perceivings. A rude instance of this: I watched a student modify her whole view of sex—I think it was sex—before my eyes when she decided in midparagraph that she was not writing for me but for her classmates. Hence a new question emerged on the rhetorical scene during the term—not, "How can one be persuasive?" but "Who is the persuader?" We didn't answer that one. In many ways I knew less about rhetoric at the end of the term than I did at the beginning, and I felt that my students, who were really very good students, might have been permanently damaged. Yet I came out happy. I felt I had relearned with new force how arbitrary and misleading are the boundaries of what we teach as rhetoric, old or new.

Let me put my new learning this way. We have a retail trade for investigation (call that scholarship) and a retail trade for rhetoric (call that Aristotle or Ramus or Brooks and Warren), but the big, unsettled, nonretail-trade problem is how the two trades interract. One can talk, as does my friend Wayne Booth, of the need for the rhetorician to *balance* his obligations to his audience and to his subject—that's a very good start, I think—but of what does the balancing consist? and how does one do it? Here, suddenly, I find great blanks in both Aristotle and Wayne Booth, and in fact in everyone writing about rhetoric except maybe Kenneth Burke, whom I can't understand. These scholars and critics may talk about balancings and interractions, but they tend to teach otherwise; they teach rhetoric as a separate, fixed thing. It is there to apply. The rhetorician masters his subject somewhere before the beginning of the rhetorical world. He then carves the subject up and gets his enthymemes out.

I was certainly not exhaustive in my search for the "new rhetoric" last term, but I did look at a number of texts that profess to bring rhetoric up to date, and what did I find? Aristotle. Aristotle forever—though sometimes with a new paint job. This was depressing. Let me cite one loaded but characteristic instance of the fixities of these texts, an instance out of Brooks and Warren's textbook, *Modern Rhetoric*. In their dealings with description (I choose description because it is the rhetorical step most closely related to the primary step of looking), Brooks and Warren take a passage from Faulkner, fix it up as an example of the undescriptive, and then give us the original as an example of the descriptive. Here are bits of the two passages:

the undescriptive: "the other waved the cigar, the other hand, in Horace's face. Horace shook it and freed his hand."

the descriptive: "the other waved the cigar, the other hand, palm up, the third finger discolored faintly at the base of a huge ring, in Horace's face. Horace shook it and freed his hand."

Now, as I say, this is a loaded instance; but I mention it because I really think it was with Faulkner's slight discoloration of the third finger that I began to want to start a new rhetoric, a rhetoric that would be a counter-rhetoric or an underground rhetoric, anyway, not our retail-trade rhetoric. (In passing, I should observe that the detail about the third finger was surely the kind that drove Nemerov straight out of novels.) I am not complaining about Faulkner but about the rhetoric text. What Brooks and Warren call "descriptive" here is literally, in the example given, a subordinate rhetorical function; that is, it is something taking place in a dependent clause in Faulkner's sentence. It is an excrescence, an ornament. And so much, Brooks and Warren seem to be saying, for description.

So much also, I infer, for looking—at least when one teaches rhetoric.

I am asserting that modern rhetoric remains largely an elaborate and fixed game of show-and-tell, a game that not only subordinates the primary step of look-and-see to a point where it is neglected, but also fails to consider at all the complicated social and psychological conditioning that affects what we see and how we see it, and then largely *governs* what we show and tell.

That's enough about rhetoric. It isn't my business here to say what a satisfactory "new rhetoric" would consist of, even if I could, or to tell you what looking-and-seeing might do for the retail-trade novel. I have used them both as instances of an old and tired marital condition that we desperately need to be unfaithful to. The old condition is not satisfactory because the world has changed around it. We know more now about how "expression" comes about than Aristotle did, and we know differently; we must therefore look into the old arts of expression and try to determine in what respects they are insufficient.

These problems are, I know, being looked into by some, particularly the linguists. The only question I have here is: Are the problems being looked into in our graduate schools in English?

That's a rhetorical question, of course. So far as I can see, our graduate schools are not looking into such problems at all except conjecturally, that is, from a safe distance, as if they were interesting problems but somebody else's problems. The graduate schools are not doing so because they remain one of the last refuges of scholasticism in the modern world. They represent our most highbrow retail trade.

I've just finished a tiny piece of research on the first one hundred applications for jobs next year in English at Carleton, and all but two of the Phd theses described in these applications looked to me, from reading their titles, to be retail trade through and through. All but two. I grant that reading titles isn't *quite* the same as reading the theses, and maybe even a thesis purporting to deal with the symbolism of "The Waste Land" will turn out to have some infidelity in it, though I doubt it. But I won't grant any more. The evidence seems to me conclusive that the thesis remains a retail-trade operation through and through, even though many more theses are now being produced on things vaguely modern than was the case a few years ago. There's a retail trade, unfortunately, in modernity too.

I'm worrying, you see, lest some morning we wake up dead. Even as we sit here, terrible things are happening to *Titus Andronicus* and "The Waste Land," and to the novel and rhetoric; but our graduate schools will be the last to find out. Do we want the social sciences to find out first? They will. So will every poet, novelist and playwright. What is worse, so will all the institutes find out, those odd organizations blooming around us on government money, doing many, many things that the graduate schools should be doing. There will be more and more of these institutes, and they will not all be summer boondoggles, and not all dedicated merely to minor problems of pedagogy, or to the teaching of that celebrated new group, the disadvantaged. If we don't watch out, we will find ourselves displaced in our own profession, displaced because our research procedures and interests seem to deny us the duty of looking at our own potful except in the ways we *have* been looking at it. Our research procedures at the highest level in our profession, I am saying, are those that were followed in that old medieval monastery I keep hearing about where all the unsustained first premises of the world began.

Now let me be outrageous and make a general suggestion. I think that among other things we should woo our enemies the social sciences. That is outrageous, but we need them (I grant they need us, but that's a different subject). But, you may say, we wooed them before, and look what happened. I agree. We had a love affair with Freudian psychology for a while, and that went away because the id and the ego kept filling our pot with jargon and cases. We also wooed the anthropologists and the Jungian people, and lo! "The Waste Land." And of course for a long time we have had an uneasy engagement with sociology over in American Studies. But for many reasons we have not been able to get on with these disciplines steadily, and we have in fact cultivated our contempt for them by choosing from their ranks just a few exotic individuals who seemed somehow really to belong to us. It never seems to have occurred to us to imagine that, for better or worse, we partly belong to them.

We do belong to them, though we don't like to think so, and though we certainly don't like to be called a science. I'll argue anyone to sleep about our affiliations over there— and I would distinguish our affiliations from our obligations, which I won't press here, our obligations as the prime interdisciplinary discipline in the humanities to do more than sit on our private disciplinary pot. Our affiliations are inescapable. For example, one simply cannot look long at problems of rhetoric and literary form as I have been doing without facing up to all sorts of complicated behavioral matters, social and psychological. And once one gets into behavior—well, do English departments have a monopoly on that? We do not. Furthermore, we do not have a monopoly, we do not even have a firm grip, on the investigative procedure or mode that our enemies have been trying to work with for a long time: induction.

But what, you may ask, about the New Criticism? Is that not inductive criticism? The question demands another lecture, but my position, not to be defended here, is that it is inductive within a closed circuit of premises, the premises conditioned by given literary forms and purposes, the induction limited to observing whether these forms and purposes have been fulfilled. It has become part of the retail trade I am complaining about, a modified scholasticism designed, say, to worry *a* lyric to death but leave lyrics generically alone. It has been most valuable; maybe it is what has kept us alive this far. But it is not, at least as I see it now practiced, nearly enough.

Let me put my complaints one other way, and then stop. I am not hoping to sell the graduate schools in English the social sciences in one easy lesson. Or sell them a new rhetoric or a new literary form. I am just saying in loud, arrogant tones to anyone in authority or near authority in our graduate schools: *Move.* Sometimes I wish I could run a graduate school in English with a free hand, oh, marvelous! Then I would issue dozens of official memoranda to the faculty on the subject of our retail trade, some of which would read as follows:

You are directed to conduct a search for the art of persuasion or effective speech, and bring it back alive.

You are directed to deny all graduate students the privilege of doing their theses on any of the fifty following literary dead ducks (supply your own list if you have one; otherwise I have several).

You are directed to arrange a collective research project into the languages of various social groups, notably sociologists, journalists, administrators, and college sophomores. And report back. Also, you are directed to begin a course or two in the study and correlation of terms in different academic departments. For example, I would like to know the difference between a romantic and a neurotic. Please throw in a few theses on these problems as you go along.

You are directed to arrange for at least a quarter of your candidates for the doctorate in English to conduct a team research project with fellow graduate students in one of the behavioral sciences.

You are directed to arrange for every graduate student in English to serve as apprentice, for a short period, to an elementary school teacher and to a high school teacher, as well as to cope with the usual freshmen.

Or, more grandly:

It has been suggested by certain colleagues in other parts of this university that a poem, a play, a novel, or an essay does not, despite all our instruction, establish in all ways and forever its own conditions for being. They assert oddly that things are in flux, and that the flux has a way of conditioning language—even our language—and literature—even the best that has been known and thought. They say crudely, rephrasing T. S. Eliot, that the best does not rest. You are requested to investigate this curious hypothesis.

So there are some of the memoranda I would issue in my graduate school. But since I don't believe in memoranda, and don't plan to run a graduate school, I suppose I am merely hoping that the proposed changes will take place automatically and mysteriously, though I know better. At any rate I have no alternative to leaving such small administrative problems to you administrators, God bless you. Innovations, I know, are in the air now, and in your heads; and a number of interesting experiments seem to be starting. But my impression is that they are being started tentatively and with great caution. We need to plan instead, in a sizable number of brave schools, a radical revision of our requirements and procedures. Each one of the brave schools should be led by a ruthless literary MacNamara to move in and knock out some of the seedier bases and navy yards, to make room for the new world—for it won't be easy. But it needs to be done soon. Let me end with a few high words on that word "soon."

Our high schools, except perhaps in the rooms with the new math, are still hanging on pretty much to education as education in everyday, traditional assumptions. Our colleges, however, are not; our colleges are changing fast. Education there is becoming increasingly an investigation of various retail trades, and sometimes quite openly an undermining of them. That is, it is becoming an education in what are sometimes called "open-field" theories of knowledge. Yet our graduate schools are still back with the high schools, in that they still address themselves to a closed field, and to mapping every square foot of it. I am not a devout open-field man, and I wouldn't want you to go away thinking I would simply destroy our field. But I'm sufficiently pragmatic and pessimistic to doubt that the graduate schools can remain aloof from the intellectual unrest of the colleges and survive long. Our roots are not so deep as we sometimes seem to think. The sublime years of our reign number around a hundred. We can be replaced as quickly as the classical disciplines were replaced, partly by us, only a short while back. Something is going on in education around us now that will doubtless be described as a revolution in a few years. It is during revolutions that old orders get replaced.

9

POETRY AND THE
SKINNER BOX

[The Bain-Swiggett Lecture at Princeton, 1967]

Mostly, Skinner Boxes have rats in them, not poets. The rats get food pellets for good behavior, electric shocks for bad. They learn the good life fast. They don't run much any more; they *are* run, by your neighborhood psychologist.

Poets are run too, of course. Up in the sky there's a big poetic equivalent of B. F. Skinner conditioning poets. My subject is modern poets in boxes, what they are being asked to do in the boxes, and by whom.

The subject is not a new one, though my analogy may be novel. The history of modern poetry is a history of poets jumping out of old boxes and thinking themselves thereby unboxed. You know that history, the history of Whitman, Pound, Williams and their many successors. You know the magic of the word "new" and the complicated life it lives with the word "old." If you are very learned, you have even read a book called *The Tradition of the New*, a title that might be converted here to *The Box of the Unboxed*. Usually, however, discussions of poets in boxes are discussions of verse forms and conventions. The battle against old forms has not been won, but it has certainly been waged. I won't wage it again here. There is no way of avoiding the forms of poetry; they are part of its life, and also come in boxes. There is no good way of separating out statements from forms. The distinguishing properties of

186

poetry—if in fact it has any that are firmly its own—are a mixed bag of properties somehow partaking of both form and statement simultaneously.

This is just an old-fashioned way of saying that the medium is the message. But McLuhan's remark is lopsided; we should at least add that the message is the medium, and then qualify endlessly. I'll do some qualifying later.

To get started with the poet's predicament in his box, I would have you imagine a genuine four-bit poet at his desk in the north woods starting to write a poem. He has just written private letters to his wife and children and his editor and his dog, and he has also just knocked off a lecture for a college audience about the life of some collective poet in a Skinner Box; and now he turns to write a poem. The question before him is what specific action he should take at that desk to shuffle off his other coils, or boxes, and reveal his lovely poetic being.

He might instantly elect to write a sonnet. Then he could turn to his notebook and ungum a few previously selected tropes from other poets, each ten metronomic syllables long. But if he prides himself on being a *modern* poet he has been conditioned against sonnets. He probably won't begin with any particular verse form in mind. Instead he will start with a notion of a role he is going to play, a stance he is going to adopt. For example, he may start by sitting at his desk in a different way than when he wrote his lecture, or by looking at the ceiling more than when he wrote his letters. We can't be sure what posturings he will go through to assert his poetitude, but we can be sure he will go through them. Otherwise, no pellets.

> Imagine me now at my desk converting this lecture to
> a poem.
> My pulse rate stays the same, though I may smoke a
> bit more.
> I see the same woods out my window that I saw before,
> And the same snow, and maybe the same crow.

And I hear the same sounds of cars and busses chugging
  through my heavily urbanized north woods,
And hear in my mind's ear the same deafening applause
From that fine audience of scholarly Princetonians
That I conjured up as I pounded out my lecture, the
  real one.
But somehow as I sit here in the obscurity of my new
  role,
I sense that the desk has changed, the woods have
  changed, the boxed world upon which I am to report
  has changed,
Changed because I have.
I am not yet committed to rhymes, though I have tried
  a couple.
I am not yet at all sure what cadence it is I am striving
  for.
I am even still halfheartedly persuaded that I can voice
  the same profundities, somehow,
That I squeezed into my lecture.
But I have changed, and therefore my subject as well
  as my form has changed.
It is a transformation that maybe my Muse arranged,
The old bitch, whoever she is.
I will call her Liz.

That's enough of the poem. I merely wanted to introduce you to Liz, the poet's B. F. Skinner. The merits
of the lines she just squeezed out of me are not my subject
here, but the nature of her demands upon me as I wrote
the lines. Obviously some of her demands are general,
applicable to *any* poem I might write. In this poem or in
any other she is sure to say that I should establish a tonal
difference between the poem and a nearly equivalent prose
statement. And she is apt to say that I should move into
the private world of the poet (though the privacy need not
be expressed in the first person), that I should make the
statement experiential as well as dialectical or rhetorical,
and that I should throw in a little music. These seem to be

the ingredients of most of my poetic transformations. But in the poem above, the Muse also insisted on a particular stance for the imagined forensic occasion of a lecture; she seems to have told me that I shouldn't be *very* poetic, somehow, but sound a *little bit* prosaic, as if I were almost lecturing but not quite.

There is no knowing what she will tell me for the next poem. She is unstable. I woke up in the middle of the night at the Nassau Club not long ago with this line coming out of my mouth:

Twenty-two tickets to Tripoli, please, said the big cheese, slowly.

Obviously the Muse sent me that line, though it's not my style. She may have thought I needed practice being Edith Sitwell or Higgledy-Piggledy. Or maybe she sent it to aggravate. I didn't know what to do with it. I thought the big cheese might be a sultan asking for twenty-one tickets for his wives, one for himself; but I didn't know why they were going to Tripoli, and I didn't care. And I didn't care why the sultan said what he said *slowly*. All I knew was that the line had been handed me. It was poetic. Liz had said so.

Many of you are familiar with M. H. Abrams' book *The Mirror and the Lamp*, and his diagram of the word "poem" in a box surrounded by three other boxes labeled "author," "universe," and "audience." The point of the diagram is to assert that a poem conducts transactions with all three. I like the diagram. Poetry is a transaction, an action between forces rather than the lonely, self-induced, self-rewarding action it is frequently made out to be. But for my purposes here I'd prefer to see the author in the middle rather than his poem. He sits there in the middle having obligations to his private poem and its medium, to the universe the poem is describing, and to an imaginary audience, that may one day be real. Now where in this diagram is the Muse? What factor is she?

The simple explanation is that she is audience. It is she who will decide on the merits of the poem's transaction with the universe. She may be a roomful of people or a reviewer or a friend; but she it is who says "yes" or "no" on the poet's transaction. "No" means no pellets.

Yet that explanation is too easy. Rhetoricians, not poets, take audiences as their muse, and even rhetoricians wrestle uneasily with themselves about the morality of working merely to win an audience. A poet is more than apt to be contemptuous of audiences. The friend, the confidant, is his best specific audience, and if the confidant reads the poem and likes it, all is well. But suppose the confidant doesn't like it. Then the poet may simply demolish the confidant. The confidant failed to see the irony of "please" in "Twenty-two tickets to Tripoli, please." He missed the contrast between the lilting quality of "twenty-two tickets" and the solemn sonorousness of "big cheese slowly." He even missed the syntax, thinking that the "slowly" applied to the speed of the cheese's speaking, not to the speed with which the tickets were to be handed out. In short he was not a good Muse. The clear implication in such moments is that there is a better Muse. But who is she?

Last year I gave a lecture about a poet in a desert that has some bearing here. The poet was me. I was in the army. I was driving through the Kasserine Pass in a jeep, alone. It was spring, 1943, and there were two crosses by the side of the road where I stopped to eat my C rations. They marked the temporary graves of a German soldier and an American soldier. My Muse came to me then, and I got back in my jeep and drove home to my outfit and wrote two poems, one about each cross.

It seemed a most isolated act of creation. I was far out of the literary swim. Nobody in the neighborhood read anything but *Stars and Stripes* and government memoranda. I wasn't sure I liked being free, but I certainly felt free.

Some years later I read a poem by Karl Shapiro that he had written in the South Pacific at about the same time. His poem and one of mine turned out to be very close. Both poems dealt with death on the edges of war, and the death of a stranger; and they both adopted a similar final attitude or stance toward that death, an ambivalent attitude balancing the heroism and senselessness of the death, but tipped toward heroism. Our last lines were almost twins.

That was the other lecture. I saw nothing mystical about my communion with Shapiro, whom I did not know in 1943. In any given culture at any given time, I was saying, the literature hangs together somehow. I was trying to distinguish between the collective qualities of First World War and Second World War poems, the kind of thing our critics do every day for their bread and butter. They note trends and forces after the fact, and they then label them and compare them. The only essential difference between my critical act and the usual one was that I was trying to reckon with those forces before the fact or at the time of the fact, that is, at the time when the poet meets the forces first and submits to them, pretty much without knowing what he is submitting to. If one thinks of the forces as audience, then that audience is vaguely the culture and the time, an *abstract* audience.

But what is an abstract audience? At this point the forces merge fuzzily with the universe as seen by the poet, and his culture, and also with the medium of poetry as it is then conceived by the poet and his culture. The more the poet stares at Liz as he is writing a poem, the bigger and trickier she gets. She it is who decides when a poem is right, and if he is in the Kasserine Pass he has good reason to think she is his girl, nobody else's. Only later does she turn out to have been Shapiro's girl too.

The Muse is all around the poet in the diagram; she is ubiquitous. She is also, at least in our time, eccentric. Not long ago she told me that if I were to write a poem against the Vietnam War I would have to do it in pidgin English. I haven't yet run across any other poets writing about the war in pidgin English, so it is possible that in this instance her instructions were to me alone. But I doubt it. I think there must be a poet in northern Alaska right now at work on one. He is writing it in pidgin English because everything he can think of saying about Vietnam has already been said about it, but said in ordinary English. Another way of making a Vietnam statement without being tiresome might be to make it while standing on one's head. Walter Lippmann hasn't tried that, or Senator Fulbright. The manner of such statements is crucial to poets; it has to be right somehow, fitting the current demands of medium, universe and audience; and yet it has also to be special, something never before heard on the face of the earth. If one is to be a poet in northern Alaska or southern New Jersey in our age of overprint, finding a distinctive position is a necessary prepoem step.

Distinctiveness. Mixed with permanence, timelessness, rightness. These requirements are ridiculously hard, but Liz has been demanding them. Let me go back a bit. My generation of poets was brought up on Eliot, Pound and Stevens. It was also brought up on I. A. Richards and Brooks and Warren and the *Kenyon Review*. It was a mixed generation with many irons in the fire, many nasty aesthetic issues dividing it, and of course many varied talents. But it was a generation pretty well committed, despite its diversity, to conceiving a poem as something self-sufficient and phoenixlike on a page in a secluded place. That conception can be thought of as aesthetic, but it is also a social conception, a conception putting the poet as man and political being aside as he writes his poem. I refer you to Pound's "Sextus Propertius" for an admirable rendering of my generation's proper poetic stance:

> Shades of Callímachus, Coan ghosts of Philetas,
> It is in your grove I would walk,
> I who come first from the clear font
> Bringing the Grecian orgies into Italy
>   and the dance into Italy.
> Who hath taught you so subtle a measure,
>   in what hall have you heard it;
> What foot beat out your time-bar,
>   what water has mellowed your whistles?
>
> Out-weariers of Apollo will, as we know, continue their
>   Martian generalities,
> We have kept our erasers in order.
> A new-fangled chariot follows the flower-hung horses;
> A young muse with young loves clustered about her
>   ascends with me into the aether, . . .
> And there is no high road to the Muses.
>
> Annalists will continue to record Roman reputations,
> Celebrities from the trans-Caucasus will belaud Roman
>   celebrities
> And expound the distentions of Empire,
> But for something to read in normal circumstances?
> For a few pages brought down from the forked hill
>   unsullied?
> I ask a wreath which will not crush my head.
>   And there is no hurry about it.
> I shall have, doubtless, a boom after my funeral. . . .

Those lines display the stance I am talking about, and also explain why I write about the Vietnam war in pidgin English. To say that there is no highroad to the muses is to say that the poet can't take the main thoroughfare of society but must go down obscure, little-traveled roads removed from the distentions of empire. Note that this places the poet out of things *before* he begins his poem, makes distinctiveness a condition of the Muse.

The generation following mine was a postwar generation, an atomic-age generation, all those things sociologists have said; and it was a generation committed to rejecting some of the prescriptions of my generation, notably our academic prescriptions for reading a poem. It, too, however, was committed to the prescriptions of Pound's "Sextus." The separateness of the poet and his poetic act from the affairs of empire was the major preliminary premise upon which poems got built. If you had to deal with the empire, you dealt with it from the seclusion of the Kasserine Pass or a Greenwich Village pad. As outsider. This meant that you couldn't expect an audience of insiders; it meant that you wouldn't find much of your poetic material on the front page of *The New York Times*; it meant that if you dealt with the modern public American scene at all, you dealt with it from a distance, presumably for the benefit of others also standing at a distance. Meanwhile, like Sextus, you imagined that eventually the distant places would be the close places; they would be demonstrated to be the primary world.

Very good. I think Marshall McLuhan would like it now if I said that the medium is the muse is the audience is the world is the message, and then maybe added the CIA for kicks. All these forces are *around* the poet as he sits in the middle of the Abrams diagram, and they do in some measure control him as he plays at being poet. He remains, however, the actor, the creator, the putter-together of their determinings. He is surrounded by forces issuing him hundreds of instructions, but he is distinct from them in being a receiver and passer on, and also, hopefully, in being somehow a discriminator between instructions.

Another word should be introduced here, "scene," a favorite of Kenneth Burke's. Audience-muse-world-medium —all these in a way add up to landscape or scene. Now think of this scene metaphorically as a large department store, the world's biggest Skinner Box. Department stores are very important for our culture. They have changed the character of shopping, but there was a yearning in the culture for them before they existed, a culture that has increasingly wanted itself to be free to shop at large. To walk through Macy's is to wander lonely as a cloud. The culture wants to wander lonely as a cloud, and thinks it can. This is an age of the floating self, the self as a comparative shopper *for* self, shopping the landscape or scene. The female shopper comes to mind first; but men also, though they don't seem to like department stores, think long and deep about what landscape they should shop to be identified with, what things they should surround themselves with. And certainly our students of both sexes are confirmed Macy-shoppers. They shop for novelties all the time, and so their elders accuse them of being faddish. The elders shouldn't complain so much; they may be more immune than the students to fads, having run through so many in their own time; but no age or sex or class is ever really immune now, and we should not think their selecting sprees trivial. It is the *act* of selecting, the shopping part, that is important. To select beards and guitars, or tweeds and pipes, or Robert Creeley and Denise Levertov, is to select the self's society, and thereby in a sense *find* the self.

Two points need to be made about this floating-self culture. First, the capacity to float is an economic novelty, a feature of the affluent society. Formerly those who could, or thought they could, float were a small segment of society. The rest were clearly *given* their scene, medium and audience, as well as their shoes and dresses. They were given them by their class and occupation. Second, the floating sensation we get while shopping is a deceptive sensation. Any advertiser will be pleased to tell you that woman A who just seemed to float up to Counter B to buy item C really did so because of the ten-billion-dollar campaign the producers of item C recently undertook. Similarly, any aging teacher of creative writing will be pleased to tell you that student A who simply floated, in poem or story, to big-city B and had lonely experience-in-a-bar C was actually led by the nose by his culture to B and C.

Such determinings are not new. Even the small segment of society that was formerly in an economic position favorable to floating has left us plenty of testimony to the anomalies of the floating condition, in the past before department stores. Take the melancholy man of Elizabethan times. He was idle and affluent, that is, *free* to be melancholy, meditative and poetic. He would sit around exploring the heavens at his own sweet pace as lesser men and committed men struggled to keep Denmark or Venice or their cobbler's bench viable. At least so the melancholy man's script read. But the script, even in those times, kept contradicting itself, informing us that the melancholy man was not really his own man. He had been born perhaps as the planet Jupiter entered the cusp of the first house; and certainly he had a black-bilious condition. In other words the Elizabethans—or the Greeks for that matter—knew that floaters didn't just float. It is oddly in our own age, an age of unprecedented interest in conditioning, that we find the wonders and virtues of floating being asserted naïvely and dogmatically, that we find floating prescribed as a way of life.

Back to poetry. Poets and students are the most dedicated floaters we have. Only this week I listened for two hours in Washington to the complaints of a group of bright high-school students against their teachers and the system. Their teachers weren't letting them float enough or shop enough or wander lonely as a cloud enough. Their teachers were asking them niggling factual questions, making them do all sorts of "busy work," not letting them get their learning on their own without pressures, exams, deadlines. Our poets go around complaining like this too. The complaints of both parties are familiar enough to all of us, and to most of us here I suspect they are complaints with which we can sympathize, for we are all—students, poets, and teachers alike—oppressed by the system's tyrannical ways. And the way of poetry has seemed to all of us an especially good way to escape the oppressions of the contemporary scene and be able to shop, as God meant us to, for ourselves.

Sextus shopped for a scene and self that he could call his own, rejecting the controls of contemporary scene—and I think his kind of shopping has been the characteristic modern kind, though each poet has wrestled in his own way with the central shopping problem of how free one *is* when shopping. Eliot's Prufrock, for example, felt much less free as a shopper than Sextus. He didn't so much choose a secluded scene as have it thrust on him. He wanted at the beginning to make the big public scene, be identified with it, even control it. But then he discovered that he wasn't up to it. He therefore retreated at the end to the private underwater dream scene he came to feel he had been fated to occupy. This is not Sextus' line at all; Sextus strongly suggests he has escaped fate by positively rejecting the big scene and positively constructing his own art scene.

Though Prufrock seems to me psychologically the sounder man, Sextus is the affirmer of artistic integrity, and of the capacity of the creative mind to escape its Skinner Box; and so he has had the idealistic shoppers on his side throughout the century.

Then there is a third kind of shopper, sitting ambiguously between Sextus and Prufrock, one who wants like Prufrock to shop the big scene but isn't frustrated like Prufrock when he does so. He comes out like Sextus affirming his freedom, but at the same time, unlike Sextus, is a public man. He is apt to be very arrogant indeed.

Pound himself assumed the public role later in his

career. He reversed his Sextus position and tried, ineffec-
tually and sadly, from the far reaches of Rapallo, to save
American democracy from usury and its consequences.
Then at the same time there was MacLeish with *his* public
period, trying to bring artists and intellectuals to public
responsibilities. MacLeish succeeded in becoming a public
man himself, as Pound did not, but he alienated his poetic
peers by doing so, as Pound did not. Furthermore, Mac-
Leish's public poems, like *America Was Promises*, had
almost no effect on the poetry following them, whereas
Pound's influence still lingers, but as a Sextus poet, not a
public poet, not a poet speaking in a forum.

   After MacLeish we had a whole decade of relatively
bookish, private poetry in the *Prufrock* mode. Here is a
sample of my own verse fitting that mode:

ALADDIN'S GENIE

The bells of the clapboard church ring; the faithful
Trudge along in the wet to their class on frailty.
The genie withdraws to his lamp; caps it. It is Sunday,
When each comes into his own,
And eats his chicken dinner and lies down.

The genie lies down. He is soft and fiftyish.
He has been smoking, drinking, having his lamp rubbed
For five thousand years.
His lungs are coated like old industrial chimneys,
The walls of his mind are plastered with grimy images,
Spells, tatters of rhetoric.
No surface is bare, the whole interior landscape
Slutted with slag, a sort of verbal New Jersey.
What a mess.

Yet year after year more and more it is there for solace.
He turns, as now,
Away from all that other, Aladdin piously
Pewed up with his Lady Badr-al-Badur,

Turns wheezing, arthritic, to his own church,
His own befouled chaos and old night,
Where some grave clinker from midst the clinkers
  beckons
And deep, fathoms of flesh down, plays him muse.

There is underwater shopping, in a jar. I read it as preliminary to saying that since the late fifties some poets—I'm not sure about myself—seem to have been coming up for air. The beats started it. The word "beats" has been discredited, so I use it only historically to describe the revolution that took place with the poem "Howl" at its center. Call that a revolution for making the private shopper a public man, or a revolution proclaiming the underwater man in the forum—at any rate it was an odd revolution to take place in a forum, but it did take place there, and left us a forum *en déshabillé,* and of course with the poets *in* the forum *en déshabillé.* It left us with engaged poets preaching disengagement, poets with an audience, with public-speaking obligations, shouting down the public. The revolution was certainly a moral and dialectical oddity, but as a scene changer it was straightforward and effective. For example, poetry reading as a genre was changed rapidly by the beats. The poet had to become a performer, and he did. He couldn't stay down in his lamp with the clinkers, but had to accept some of the obligations of a rhetorician, and he did. In other words his audience-scene changed dramatically, and the change could only change his stance as a poet and his statements themselves.

Now let me describe a recent affair in Texas where this scene change for poetry readings was evident, and where also the original role of the beats—publicly preaching the unpublic—was modified. The scene was an enormous meeting of English teachers in Houston, a meeting of the National Council of Teachers of English. A dozen miscellaneous poets of different ages and dispensations were invited there to read their poems in various cubbyholes of a large convention hotel.

Most of the poets arrived annoyed that they had been scheduled to compete with one another. The program began with a large collective meeting in a ballroom. Richard Eberhart, one of our dozen, started the ceremonies with a speech praising all kinds of poetry from all kinds of people. He made creativity indiscriminately grand. Then the authorities on stage, trying to wind up the ballroom event, neglected to introduce the other poets individually. We were sitting in the front row waiting to be introduced. When we weren't, we started shouting. That started the new world.

Some of us rose to complain about the Eberhart speech. He had maligned the sternness and integrity of poetry, we said, making it a namby-pamby all-around good thing like Wheaties and democracy. And others of us rose shouting to say that we should each be allowed to read an introductory poem to the big audience before being shipped off to smaller rooms. We were eloquent and loud. The teachers were fascinated. In half an hour our dozen, with Eberhart concurring, had formed a team to fight the Establishment.

We reorganized our own program. Then we performed in gangs for the rest of the day. We not only read poems but also talked and talked about Vietnam and dirty words and teaching. The teachers didn't get the simple vision of the creative life they had bargained for, with rhymes and images and running brooks. They got a disturbance, and most of them seemed to like it. It was an authoritative disturbance (a dozen live poets), and it was a breath of fresh air. English-teacher meetings are not known for their fresh air.

Never had I seen a group of poets act like this. Where

were our withdrawal symptoms? Such a scene would have
been impossible before the beats, and yet it was also somehow a progression from or out of the beats. The audience
for beats had always been *more* beats, but the audience in
Texas was high-school English teachers, that is, an audience
firmly representing a part of the Establishment that the
beats had noisily withdrawn from.

Establishments are in trouble all around these days,
and the English Establishment sometimes seems to lead all
the rest in trouble. As a result it has been casting around
for ways of reforming itself, keeping up to date. It too has
been shopping. It has been shopping with staid educational
reformers, with wild men like Leslie Fiedler and Paul
Goodman, and with discontented students. It was shopping
in Texas. It was looking for help when it brought the
poets in.

Poets have been sitting around "in residence" in the
halls of ivy for years, and for years they have mostly bick-
ered about whether they, delicate flowers, could survive on
campus. But in Texas the scene was different. Lurking in
the air was the new question of whether the Establishment
could survive. For, rightly or wrongly, the Establishment
now has an inferiority complex; and the poets, having had
their innings with integration and Vietnam, are full of
beans. And for a day in Texas they were the public men on
the public scene, the reformers of education.

But how would they reform it? To carry a sign against
Vietnam or to go on an anti-Vietnam poetry-reading junket
on a float behind a truck is a brave and even dangerous
gesture at reform, but a gesture only dimly related to the
Houston problem of dealing directly with Establishment
procedures and persons. Poets, even our most reformist
poets, have steered clear of political engagement in this
sense; they have not been distinguished for their prag-
matism, with the "how" of reform. In Texas, faced with

the educational Establishment, they had an unusual audience and an unusual opportunity for the anarchist—and it is in this sense that I mean they were in a new world.

As an aside, I remember coming back from the war in 1945, and then spending a year here at Princeton, and then going out still full of the war to a little town in Minnesota to teach. The Bomb had fallen; the UN spirit was everywhere in that town; it was hard to get a quorum together to acknowledge the existence of gunpowder. And right away I found myself surrounded by a little nest of academic-wifely-type pacifists. Soldiering was still so much a part of my mental scene that I kept thinking what fools those women were, in that little town with their big programs.

I had something of the same feeling in Texas. In a way we poets were the fools in town with the big program. The odd thing was that this time the fools weren't alone; the Establishment was there listening, and behind them were all those thousands of students who have been listening in late years to the poets. Here then was a scene change for poets and other fools. Could it not presage a change in the character of the foolery?

Well, that question is still around, and it will be answered by time, not by Bain-Swiggett lecturers or by any of the poets who were in Texas. After all, the scene change in Texas was a momentary change, and a change affecting the Skinner-Box lives of only twelve poets. I mention it only as a possibly significant symptom of change. Yet for us twelve poets the Texas affair changed forever, if only slightly, our stance as poets at our desks. For us, Texas changed slightly our medium, and hence changed slightly any future message we might write in it.

If Texas is followed for us by similar public engagements, the Muse may well come to recommend to each poet that he move out of his lamp with the clinkers, and also move out of his tight little world of other poets, other artists. Such a recommendation sounds fine to me in an abstract way; I have thought for a long time that poets should spend fewer hours in towers and confessional boxes, stop making easy and glib connections between their private troubles and the world's, stop worrying so much about stance and style. In other words, I have thought idly for a long time that the nasty little selves of poets should be deflated, but I haven't been able to do anything about it, even for my own nasty little self.

Perhaps this is the chief point I have to make about our Skinner-Box life, that we do not control it, or control much of it. We simply cannot decide on our own that we will turn over a new leaf and get engaged. We cannot will such changes, as MacLeish long ago seemed to think we could. The Muse, as I have laboriously defined her, does most of the willing.

If we omit from our considerations the overwhelming problem of what poets *ought* to write or do, we might, I think, be better off as critics. At least it would be good for us to take a short vacation from the "ought." When I try to do this with reference to the Texas affair and what it may do to change poetic statement in some vague sociological way, I come up with two possibilities—first, that poets and their poetry will become wildly aggressive in the next few years, seeking to dominate nice little Establishment people like English teachers; or second, that they will become beautifully humble and sweet. But in either event, my Skinner self tells me I should be calm and unmoral. The event will be determined in large measure by my Muse.

The triumph of the domination impulse is a good bet, I'm afraid. The old Sextus-Propertius withdrawal theme converts very readily to its opposite—from "poets are the true legislators of the world when all those Romans get out of the way" to "poets are the true legislators now." Get those high-school teachers in line. Get them to teach all their students to be shopper-poets, shopping for their selves, their private truths. Take advantage of your new role, Sextus, and make the world over in your image.

Humility seems craven. What poet wants the National Council of Teachers of English to write his poems for him? And why should he retreat from authority when for the first time authority is potentially in his hands?

Yet the triumph, such as it was, in Houston was mixed with doubt, I think, for most of us. Perhaps I should speak only for myself, but I think others there shared with me the uneasiness of preaching the virtues of self and the spontaneous, free shopping life, while remembering urgently the hell of self, and the hell of always asserting the self, which has been the poet's special hell in our time. To me at least it seemed that the Muse might be whispering for us to get down on our knees to those high-school teachers.

Yet I wasn't sure. I think I would have preferred to get down on my knees to a G.I. or a small bureaucrat. The Muse wasn't really letting me out of my box by giving me English teachers. I am disappointed in her still, and upset as much as pleased by Houston. I still don't know what to make of her.

I haven't written a single poem since Houston, which is maybe what I make of her. The paradoxes are rolling in fast.

If to find the self one must lose the self, then perhaps to find the poetry one must stop the poetry; to be distinctive one must be indistinct; to be saved one must be damned; and to conquer the scene or box that surrounds and determines, one must be a perfectly obedient, uncreative rat.

As a final aside let me observe that this struggle between opposites, so familiar and old a part of our literary heritage, is also an old anxiety-dream struggle, what I will call the limbo dream. You are in the middle, you are shuttling, one force keeping you from the other, delaying you, keeping you from your identity, your wholeness. Its sexual implications are many and complex, but so are its aesthetic implications. The other night, at 3:00 A.M., I was caught between a dinner party with friends, whose identities kept changing, and an evening class. There was the trouble, first, of getting away from the dinner, followed by problems with cars and large parking lots; and then I found myself at the place of the class, but alone and stuck with two cars, one of which I was obliged to return to the party before I could attend the class. Suddenly the whole problem was transformed, and I had two full milk bottles, one small, one large, and the obligation (note that the obligation persists) to fit the one inside the other.

I did. I put the big milk bottle on its side, opened the trap door in its side and put the little milk bottle in. Unfortunately, by then it was too late to make the class.

I don't know what I am saying, but I hope the Muse is listening. After all, it was she who concocted this box, this limbo.

INDEX